INTE
Planning, Assessment, and Improvement in Higher Education

BARBARA J. SHERLOCK, EDITOR

NACUBO

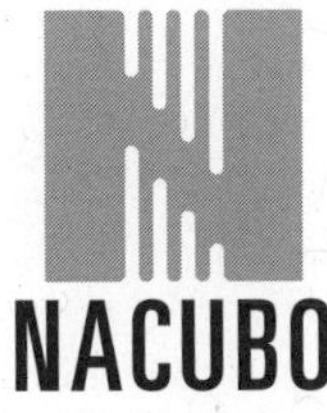

Library of Congress Cataloging-in-Publication Data

Integrating planning, assessment, and improvement in higher education / Barbara J. Sherlock, editor.
p. cm.
ISBN 978-1-56972-049-3
1. Universities and colleges--United States--Administration. 2. Education, Higher--United States--Planning. 3. Educational planning--United States--Evaluation. 4. School improvement programs--United States. I. Sherlock, Barbara J. II. National Association of College and University Business Officers.
LB2341.I545 2009
378.1'07--dc22

2009021934

NACUBO saved the following resources by using Rolland Enviro 100 paper (FSC certified 100% post-consumer fiber, certified EcoLogo, processed chlorine free, FSC recycled, and manufactured using biogas energy) and New Leaf Reincarnation Matte (designated Ancient Forest Friendly and manufactured with electricity that is offset with Green-e®certified renewable energy certificates, 100% recycled fiber and 50% post-consumer waste, and processed chlorine free: 8 fully grown trees, 5,047 gallons of water, 535 pounds of solid waste, 1,039 pounds of air emissions, 3.4 pounds of suspended particles in the water, and 1,226 cubic feet of natural gas. Calculations based on research by Environmental Defense and other members of the Paper Task Force.

Design by Colburnhouse

National Association of College and University Business Officers
Washington, DC
www.nacubo.org

Printed in the United States of America

CONTENTS

ACKNOWLEDGMENTS

While I wrote many of the articles in this book, did the compilation, and am responsible for any deficiencies in the resulting collection, I must first thank Ann Dodd, Carol Everett, Marianne Guidos, and Louise Sandmeyer, who also contributed to this collection.

I would also like to thank the entire staff in the Office of Planning and Institutional Assessment at Penn State—Michael Dooris, Ellen George, Marianne Guidos, Virginia Hosterman, Daniel Nugent, Louise Sandmeyer, and Nicholas Warcholak—for their ongoing editorial feedback and production support,

My thanks also to NACUBO for giving Penn State the opportunity to share this information more widely then we have been able to in the past via the Web and conferences.

Louise Sandmeyer was a valuable coach throughout the development of this book.

Finally, my thanks to my husband Harold for his support throughout the process.

It is my hope that this compilation gives you insight into how these processes really work, without overwhelming you with Nittany Lion pride.

ABOUT THE EDITOR

Barbara Sherlock is a planning and improvement associate in Penn State University's Office of Planning and Institutional Assessment. The office provides facilitation and consulting services, institutional research and analysis, and educational and networking opportunities to support planning, improvement, and assessment initiatives at the unit and university level.

Ms. Sherlock previously served in the United States Navy, including as executive officer of Penn State's NROTC unit, as a consultant in the Navy's organizational development program, and in command, attaining the rank of Commander. She co-edited *To Get The Job Done: Readings in Leadership and Management* (2nd ed.) for Naval Institute Press.

Ms. Sherlock served as a Pennsylvania Quality Examiner, and as an Examiner and Judge for the Central Pennsylvania Quality Award. She earned a B.A. in Psychology from Wellesley College, an M.B.A. from Pepperdine University, and an M.S. in Computer Science from the Naval Postgraduate School. Ms. Sherlock is also a Credentialed Facilitator of Essential Lifestyle Person Centered Planning. She has shared her experiences and approaches in facilitating planning and improvement at conferences sponsored by the National Consortium for Continuous Improvement in Higher Education (NCCI), Society for College and University Planning (SCUP), and International Association of Facilitators (IAF).

INTRODUCTION

Penn State's planning and improvement efforts can be traced back to 1983, when then Penn State president Bryce Jordan began a strategic planning initiative that continues to this day. The university embarked on its quality improvement and innovation journey in the fall of 1991 with the establishment of the University Council on Continuous Quality Improvement (UCCQI) to facilitate improvement initiatives within budget units and across the university.

In 1992, UCCQI established the Continuous Quality Improvement (CQI) Center to support a culture of continuous improvement through a focus on service to stakeholders, process improvement, and data-based decision making. Over the next few years, the center worked with administrative and academic units to identify, define, and clarify critical processes; developed training (and by 1996 delivered CQI training to 5,385 faculty and staff across the university); maintained a support network for CQI team facilitators and leaders; partnered with DuPont and IBM to enhance capabilities; and worked with a volunteer planning team to hold the first Quality Expo in 1993. During this time the UCCQI commissioned the 1996 Faculty-Staff Survey, repeated in 2000, 2004, and 2008 to identify areas for improvement. The resulting data led to Penn State's certificate leadership and management professional development programs (Office Professional, Mastering SuperVision, Management Institute, Leadership Academy) and to a revision of the Staff Review and Development Plan.

In 1996 the CQI Center merged with the Office of Planning and Analysis to become the Center for Quality and Planning (CQP). This was followed in 1997 by Penn State's first university-wide strategic plan, developed by the University Planning Council (UPC), in 1998 by the UPC and UCCQI's development of 27 university-wide strategic planning indicators, and in 1999 by collaboration among the CQP, University Budget Office, Office of Physical Plant, Enrollment Management, and Commonwealth Operations to develop an integrated planning model incorporating enrollment, staffing, facilities, budget, and academic planning.

In 2003 the name of the CQP was changed to its current name, the Office of Planning and Institutional Assessment, to more accurately reflect the services the office provides. The office continues to provide assistance to units involved in planning and process improvement and innovation. As this manuscript is prepared for publication in spring 2009, 861 known CQI teams have been formed and listed in the Team Database maintained by the office. Quality Expos were held annually from 1993 through 2002; in 2003 the format was changed to the Quality Issues Forum, but the goal remains the same—to annually recognize those who contribute to innovation and improvement at Penn State.

As the office evolved, so did our means of sharing information with others. Initially we presented stand-up training and provided two-inch notebooks of reference materials to new CQI team members. Our first published material was Leading for Continuous Improvement, published in 1999 as a stand-alone reference for those considering starting a CQI team. We wrote it because we realized that those interested in starting a team would not be reaching that decision just when we happened to be offering that workshop each semester, and even if they were, they were likely to be senior leaders who would not be able to give up three hours of their time for the workshop.

In 2001 we wrote the first of what we referred to then as "four-pagers," because that was how long the first few papers were. After we wrote two or three, we realized that the series needed a name, and we decided on *Innovation Insights*. We were also able to more clearly separate what went into our newsletter, *Quality Endeavors,* and what material was more appropriate for *Innovation Insights.* Material published in *Quality Endeavors* was focused on events and accomplishments in quality and planning at Penn State. An *Innovation Insight* was written as we saw a need for a reference on a particular topic. As we did more consulting and facilitation, and less stand-up training, we also wanted reference material that would be easier to refer to than slides from a workshop, and we converted material from several workshops into *Innovation Insights*.

Around 2005, as we posted more *Innovation Insights* on the Web, we began receiving inquiries from other universities and several nonprofit health care organizations, in both the United States and Canada, asking if they could use particular *Innovation Insights* in their internal CQI training.

These requests led us to consider publishing the set of *Innovation Insights* as a book. The result, *Integrating Planning, Assessment, and Improvement in Higher Education,* will help higher education leaders as they strive to improve operations on their campuses, and design and implement their own planning or improvement initiatives.

We plan to continue to write new *Innovation Insights* when we see a need. Check out our Web site at http://psu.edu/president/pia and see what we've added.

INTEGRATING PLANNING, ASSESSMENT, AND IMPROVEMENT

SECTION I

INTEGRATING PLANNING, ASSESSMENT, AND IMPROVEMENT

How can an organization decide which goals and strategies to include in a plan? How can specific strategies be implemented? While it's generally accepted that there is value in planning, one of the most common complaints made about plans is that they are written and placed on a shelf. This book introduces a five-step model used for integrating planning, assessment, and improvement, and includes data sources and tools for each step of the process. A survey that can be used to assess performance is also included.

BACKGROUND

Many organizations use planning, improvement, and assessment to help their organization advance and succeed. Developing plans, whether for one to three years or fifteen to twenty, is an accepted and expected organizational activity. Process improvement is practiced to increase efficiency, effectiveness, and returns on limited resources. Assessing or measuring performance indicates how well an organization is doing. But often, within a single organization, these activities are undertaken separately, with no communication or feedback that would make it possible for one activity to support, reinforce, or enable the other. Penn State's model for integrating planning, assessment, and improvement moves plans off the shelf and into the weekly and daily scheduling and prioritizing process. It uses assessment as a guide for future actions and goals, and process improvement, innovation, and reengineering as a means to implement a plan.

THE BASIC MODEL

Integrating planning, assessment, and improvement is a continuous process that includes data from many sources. It begins with Step 1, a data-based assessment of the current state of the organization. This is followed by Step 2, in which the organization develops, confirms, or updates its mission, vision, and goals. In Step 3, the unit identifies measures for each of the goals and related outcomes. Then, by examining the gaps between where the organization is and where it wants to be, based on the data collected and the measures developed earlier, in Step 4 the organization prioritizes its strategies and actions. Finally, in Step 5, the unit uses teams and traditional innovation and improvement tools to implement the identified strategies and actions. This brings the organization back to the start of the process, to assess progress toward the goals in their plan. This process is illustrated in the basic model below.

Figure 1.1—The Penn State Model: Integrating Planning, Improvement, and Assessment

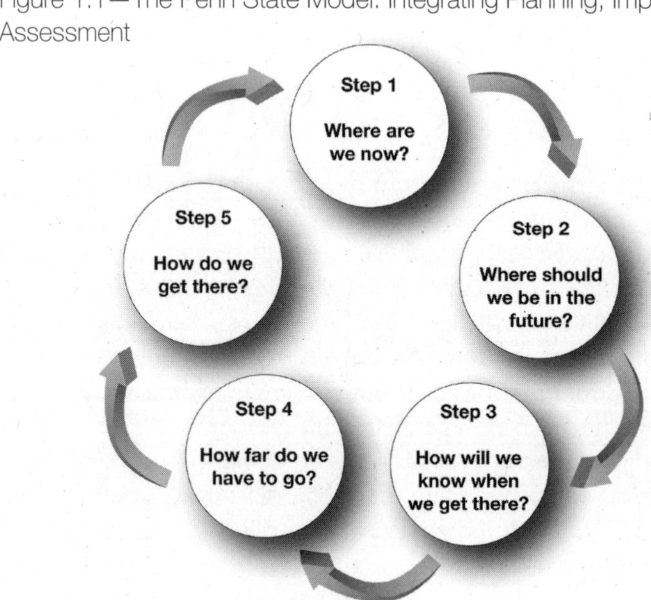

A more detailed discussion follows of each step in the model and tools to facilitate each step. Citations for each tool are listed in the reference section.

THE FIVE STEPS AND RELATED TOOLS

Step 1: Where are we now?

For those who are updating a plan, or who developed a plan in the past, Step 1 begins with a review of the progress toward goals in the previous plan, and any information regarding reasons for progress being made or not made.

The next task is to identify what is changing and what trends are having an impact on the organization, both internally and externally. Additionally, there should be clarification of the identity of the organization's stakeholder groups—those who have an interest, either directly, because they are receiving the unit's service or product, or indirectly, because they are impacted by the unit's actions—and how well the organization is meeting each stakeholder group's expectations. Finally, the organization needs to identify its strengths, core competencies, and capacity for growth and development.

Data Sources and Tools for this Step

The first source for information to determine the current state of the unit is any data collected as part of a *recent assessment* process. Annual *unit performance data*, and any insight provided by information from an *institutional data warehouse* is also useful. *Surveys, interviews,* and *focus groups* can be used to gather information about stakeholder satisfaction, expectations, and thoughts about trends. Review of the *media* may also provide insight on trends.

Step 2: Where should we be in the future?

At this point, the organization needs to look at what it is currently doing and determine what it should be doing more, less, or none of in the future. Also, what should it be doing that it is not doing now? What are stakeholders expecting or looking for? In what direction is the larger organization moving, and how can the unit align with or support that? How can the unit support and further the core mission of the organization? In this step the organization can develop or refine its mission, vision, and goals, if necessary.

Data Sources and Tools for this Step

Information from *surveys, interviews,* and *focus groups* conducted as part of Step 1 can feed into this step. *Affinity diagrams* can be used to cluster individual expectations and possibilities into specific goal or strategy categories. *Scenario planning* can be used to assess trends and identify possible future scenarios that the plan can prepare for or anticipate.

Step 3: How will we know when we get there?

One of the key components of a dynamic plan is measures to indicate progress. These performance indicators should align with mission, vision, and goals to indicate the rate at which the organization is moving toward its goals. However, the emphasis should be on data that can be gathered with minimal overhead, and as part of normal operations. Measurement should not consume more resources than the data it produces is worth.

Data Sources and Tools for this Step

The unit should first look at the *data it already collects* and see whether, or how, any of this can be used to assess progress. *Benchmarking* may be a useful way to determine what measures similar units use. However, the key here is to benchmark processes and approaches, and not use the data collected as a means of comparing performance with other units. If new data must be collected, *brainstorming* and *multivoting* may be a means of getting group input on all of the possibilities, and then narrowing down the possibilities to the most efficient and effective.

Step 4: How far do we have to go?

Once the unit has determined how to measure performance, has baseline data for current performance, and has performance goals, it can determine how much effort will be required to attain each goal.

Not all initiatives can, should, or need to be started at once. In Step 4, the unit can determine with which strategies or initiatives it wants to start, based on available resources, cost, timing, logical sequence, or some other criteria. Those not selected for immediate action are not forgotten. They are just put aside until progress has been made on the selected set of actions. This list of possible future initiatives should be revisited on a quarterly, semi-annual, or annual basis.

Data Sources and Tools for this Step

A *radar chart* may help determine which issues drive others in the organization, and thus where actions should begin and what will produce the greatest return. A *gap analysis* will provide information on the resources and actions needed to get from the current situation to the desired future state. A *prioritization matrix* provides a means to evaluate alternative actions in terms of predetermined criteria.

Step 5: How do we get there?

The final step in the model involves actual implementation of initiatives. Without implementation of initiatives to produce changes, the document is just another plan sitting on the shelf. At this step, it is necessary to identify who will be involved in implementing each initiative, and what resources they will need.

Data Sources and Tools for this Step

Many of the tools used in traditional improvement teams apply here. First, having a *team* address the initiative will increase the likelihood of support for the change by those in the unit. It will also ensure a wider perspective in determining how to implement the initiative. In improving or reengineering an already existing process, *process mapping* or *flowcharting* will document the current process and help identify functions that must be retained, even if the way the function is done changes. A *fishbone* or *Ishikawa diagram* will help identify problem areas in the current process. Finally, a *responsibility matrix* or *planning grid* will document what actions are needed to implement the initiative, and who will do what when. The more detailed model, with tools that may be used at each step, is shown on the next page.

Figure 1.2—The Penn State Model: Integrating Planning, Improvement, and Assessment: A Model and Tools

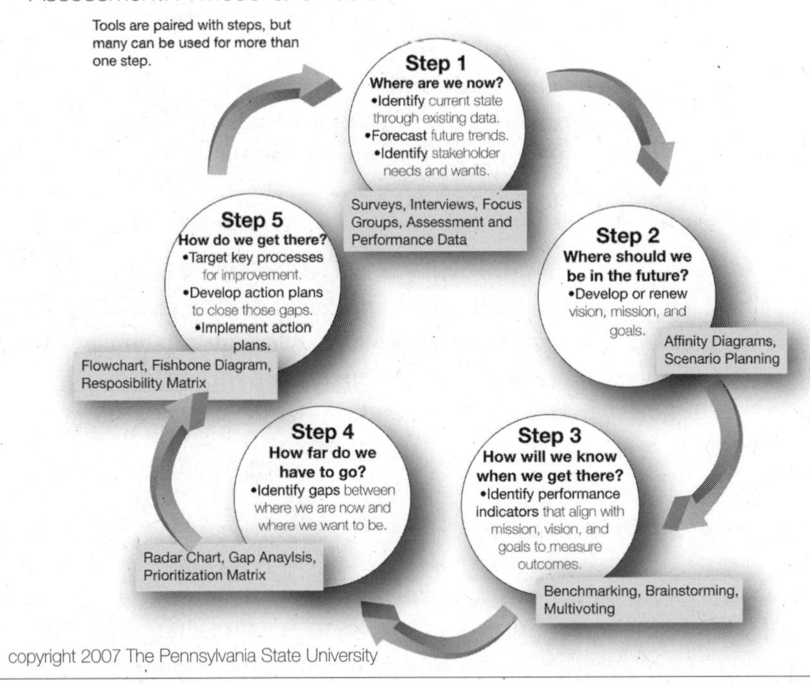

NEXT STEPS

Once the organization develops a plan and begins implementation, monitoring of progress should occur on a regular, scheduled basis—quarterly, semi-annually, or annually. As implementation of the highest priority initiatives is completed, the list of remaining initiatives can be updated and reprioritized, based on the evolving environment, and the new top priority initiatives can be implemented. At some point, it will be appropriate not just to reprioritize initiatives, but also to formally reassess the current situation and coming trends, beginning the cycle again.

Your Unit's Integration of Planning, Assessment, and Improvement Activities

The brief survey on the following pages will provide a snapshot of where your unit is in integrating its planning, assessment, and improvement activities. You may want to think of this as another assessment tool in your unit's toolkit—something that will provide information about how to refine and enhance current planning, assessment, and improvement activities. For areas where you answer "Yes," maintain and improve current activities. For areas where you are "Not Sure," check to find out what information is available and what you need to close the gaps. For areas where you are sure your answer is "No," determine what your first steps should be to address the issue. With these answers, you will be in a position to begin a more informed planning, assessment, and improvement process.

REFERENCES

Bens, Ingrid. (1999). *Facilitation at a Glance! Your Pocket Guide to Facilitation*. Cincinnati, OH: AQP and Participative Dynamics. (Gap Analysis)

Brassard, M. (1989). *The Memory Jogger Plus +*. Methuen, MA: GOAL/QPC. (Prioritization Matrix)

Brassard, M. and D. Ritter. (1994). *The Memory Jogger II: A Pocket Guide of Tools for Continuous Improvement & Effective Planning*. Methuen, MA: GOAL/QPC. (Radar Chart, Prioritization Matrix)

Goal/QPC-Oriel, Inc. (1995). *The Team Memory Jogger: A Pocket Guide for Team Members*. Madison, WI: Oriel.

Lindgren, M. and Bandhold, H. (2003). *Scenario Planning: The Link Between Future and Strategy*. New York, NY: Palgrave Macmillan.

Office of Planning and Institutional Assessment. (2006). Innovation Insights #4: Benchmarking for Innovation and Improvement. http://www.psu.edu/president/pia/innovation/. University Park, PA: The Pennsylvania State University.

Ibid. Innovation Insights #8: How to Use Focus Groups to Solicit Ideas and Feedback. http://www.psu.edu/president/pia/innovation/.

Ibid. (2005). Innovation Insights #11: Assessing for Improvement. http://www.psu.edu/president/pia/innovation/.

Ibid. (2006). Innovation Insights #12: Tools for Organizational IMPROVEment. http://www.psu.edu/.president/pia/innovation/(Brainstorming, Multivoting, Affinity Diagram, Flowcharting/Process Mapping, Fishbone/Ishikawa Diagram, Responsibility Matrix).

Ibid. (2006). Innovation Insights #14: Using Surveys for Data Collection in Continuous Improvement. http://www.psu.edu/president/pia/innovation/.

Scholtes, P. R, Joiner, B., and Streibel, B. (1996). *The Team Handbook: How to Use Teams to Improve Quality 2nd ed.* Madison, WI: Joiner Associates Inc. (Planning Grid)

Scholtes, P.R. (1998). *The Leader's Handbook*. New York, NY: McGraw-Hill.

Where Is Your Unit in Integrating Planning, Assessment, and Improvement?

Your response to this profile will give you a quick snapshot of where your work unit is in the process of integrating planning, assessment, and improvement initiatives. Each section of the profile relates to one of the steps in the five-step model for integrating planning, assessment, and improvement. For each question, indicate whether you can or cannot answer the question, or are not sure. You don't need to provide a detailed answer to each question to complete the survey.

	Yes	No	Not Sure
Step #1: Where are you now?			
Do you know…			
If you have achieved the goals you set in the last planning cycle?			
If there are goals you haven't achieved, and what the reasons are?			
What changes have occurred in your unit since you implemented your last plan?			
In the institution?			
In your discipline/profession?			
What social, economic, political trends are impacting your unit?			
To your advantage?			
To your disadvantage?			
Who your current stakeholders are? What their expectations are for the services you provide? If there have been changes in their expectations?			
How well you are meeting their expectations?			
What your current capacity is for growth/development?			
What your core competencies are? What you do well?			
Who your external partners are? Who your competitors are? How well you and they are doing?			

	Yes	No	Not Sure
Step #2: Where should you be in the future?			
Do you know…			
What your unit would look like in x years if you were best in the delivery of…?			
How you are adding value in support of the University's core mission?			
What your stakeholders will be expecting from you and how you will be meeting those expectations?			
What core values you have preserved?			
What you will be doing differently?			
More of? Less of?			
Step #3: How will you know when you get there?			
Do you know…			
What you are currently measuring? What the data tell you about how you are currently performing?			
What great performance would look like? Who your benchmarks are?			
How your measures map to your goals and to your stakeholders' expectations?			
If there are measures you should add/ measures you should delete?			
Step #4: How far do you have to go?			
Do you know…			
What the gaps are between where you are now and where you want to be?			
What your approach is for closing these gaps?			
What the implications are for enrollment planning, staffing patterns, space, facilities, and information technology requirements?			
What budgetary and other resources you will need to close the gap?			

	Yes	No	Not Sure
Step #5: How do you get there?			
Do you know…			
What is strategically important to improve, based on your aim for the future, your stakeholder knowledge, and the internal and external environment?			
What the significant few processes are that should be targeted for improvement that will give you the greatest leverage?			
How you currently measure process performance?			
What additional information you need to determine how the process is performing to meet stakeholder expectations?			
Who the process owners are?			
Who should be involved in the redesign?			
What your implementation strategy is?			

CREATING A CULTURE FOR INNOVATION AND IMPROVEMENT

This chapter is adapted from "Creating a Culture for Continuous Improvement: Lessons Learned," the keynote presentation given by Louise Sandmeyer, Executive Director, Office of Planning and Institutional Assessment, The Pennsylvania State University, at the Advancing Improvement and Innovation conference on October 15, 2008, at the University of Virginia.

While the focus in improvement and innovation is often on tools and skills, and using a well-known or named approach, a key part of the success in implementing initiatives is paying attention to the "soft skills." To successfully implement a change, people in the organization need to be engaged and a part of the change. In our experience at Penn State, working across the university and its component units, we have found that successful innovation and improvement initiatives share several fundamental cultural components.

LINK CHANGE INITIATIVES TO WHAT MATTERS MOST

Continuous Quality Improvement (CQI) can't be an end in itself. As a means to an end, it must be tied to the larger goals of the organization—for example, achieving academic excellence, reducing bureaucracy, saving money, or increasing satisfaction. Innovation and improvement approaches can be a means to accomplish strategies and tactics in organizational plans. Focus on using improvement and innovation to move the organization where it wants to be. This generates more energy than using improvement and innovation to fix problems. Having a future-oriented perspective, talking about leadership and vision, can link individuals to the organization and add meaning to their work as they help it move forward.

THE ORGANIZATIONAL SYSTEM GETS THE RESULTS IT IS DESIGNED TO GET

If you want to change the results, you need to change the system. As the saying goes, "If you always do what you've always done, you'll always get what you've always gotten." Look at what the organization enables, rewards, and recognizes. What is the basis for performance evaluation? Don't try to tinker at the edges, and don't try to get the people to change without changing the core of the system. Remove the barriers to quality, innovation, and improvement. Change the structure to accommodate the new behaviors you desire. Integrate CQI into the core processes of the institution—how you hire, what you reward, what you communicate, how you measure, and how you develop faculty and staff. What gets measured is what gets done, and what's funded and rewarded is what's valued. Reward successful implementation of the changes you seek.

QUALITY IS EVERYBODY'S BUSINESS

Leadership needs to provide and show support for the initiatives by conveying that they are important, worth investing in, and worthy of the time it will take for their implementation. At the same time, those who are closest to the processes being addressed should be included. They know what works and where the problems are. They also will have to implement the changes and make them work. Customers and stakeholders should also have input. The organization is there to efficiently use resources to provide consumers with a service or product. The organization needs input from customers to effectively meet their needs. Surveys or focus groups are two ways to gather information about what customers are looking for, or what dissatisfies them.

THERE IS NO ONE BEST APPROACH: BE RESPONSIVE AND FLEXIBLE

Honor organizational history and tradition. Recognize the complexity and diversity within higher education. Understand how university systems operate. There are numerous models and vocabularies for implementing change. A common language can be helpful, but like CQI itself, it's a tool to an outcome, not an end in itself.

There are also individual cultures within organizational subunits. Individuals in those units are at different levels of readiness for change. Recognize all of these variables, start at the group's readiness level, and design the approach to fit. Specifically:

- Start where there is interest in beginning an improvement initiative.
- Nurture and support your "early adopters," the scouts and pioneers.
- Don't make the initiative any more complicated than it needs to be.
- Look for and include improvements that can be quick successes. Make the first initiatives small enough in scope that the group will be able to see results in a reasonable amount of time.
- Balance the amount of change and stability. Give one round of change enough time to become established before you introduce another.

COMMUNICATE AND CELEBRATE SUCCESS

Don't argue the language of quality; engage in real discussions about improvement. Meet people where they are, not where you think they should be, and give them what they need, not what you think they should have. Be able to show people and units what's in it for them.

Recognize participants' work. Celebrate the success in a timely manner. That will provide the energy to move on to longer or more complex projects, and will draw more people into the improvement process.

Share information about improvements throughout the organization. Sharing learning may trigger ideas for additional related improvement opportunities. It will also demonstrate that the organization is serious about moving in this direction and committing resources to improvement, innovation, and change.

ADAPT AND EVOLVE: STAY FOCUSED ON THE LONG-TERM VISION AND GOALS

As your approaches to innovation and improvement become established, monitor how the organization, environment, and world around you is adapting and evolving. As the organization becomes more mature in dealing with improvement and innovation, your approaches also need to mature. What's important is that the organization continues to grow as a learning and adapting organization, that it not be wedded to any one approach. Focus on the outcomes and results. Limit the focus on how it was done to lessons learned for future initiatives.

Listen to the organizational leadership. Keep the momentum going by focusing on long-term goals, listening to all of the organization's stakeholders, both internal and external, and monitoring the pulse of the organization.

WEAVE INNOVATION AND IMPROVEMENT INTO THE CULTURE OF YOUR ORGANIZATION

The goal of improvement and innovation is not the number of improvement initiatives that have been started. It is a more effective and efficient learning organization. Incorporating the cultural concepts above, and appreciating the balance between order and change, will make improvement and innovation a part of how people think on a daily basis, and help you move your organization toward its vision and goals.

THE LINK BETWEEN BEING STUDENT-CENTERED AND CONTINUOUS QUALITY IMPROVEMENT

How do Continuous Quality Improvement (CQI) principles and practices contribute to a student-centered institution? The four components of quality improvement—focusing on service to stakeholders, studying processes, making decisions based on data, and collaborating through teamwork—can be used to create, enhance, and reinforce a student-centered environment. This chapter discusses these components and provides examples of how each can be implemented.

SERVING STAKEHOLDERS

First and foremost, continuous improvement places at the heart of its efforts addressing and exceeding the needs and expectations of stakeholders. Higher education institutions have many stakeholders, including but not limited to students, parents, faculty, staff, alumni, and residents of the local community and of the state. While the institution works to address the interrelated expectations of all stakeholders, learning and student life are often the key drivers behind improvement initiatives.

Colleges and departments should conduct program reviews to ensure development of relevant and vibrant undergraduate majors. A career services program can enhance the benefits provided to students, through strengthening relationships with prospective

"...being a student-centered university also means being an employee-centered university, an alumni-centered university, a donor-centered university, and a parent-centered university. Why? Because being eager to come to work each day, going the extra mile for a student, enjoying teaching, wanting to be financially generous to one's alma mater, and being proud of your child's college choice are all related to the climate fostered by a student-centered university."

Penn State President Graham Spanier

employers, establishing an online employer database, and increasing efficiency of services. Technology makes it possible for students to develop an online e-Portfolio to represent their accomplishments.

MAKING DECISIONS BASED ON DATA

A key component of CQI is that decisions and improvements are based on data, not opinion. Telephone and online surveys can provide valuable feedback from students on topics such as academic integrity, civility, diversity, hazing, first-year experience, post-graduation plans, relationship violence, religious and spiritual services, safety, student drinking, and student satisfaction.

Surveys may also be used to obtain feedback from faculty and staff on organizational climate and satisfaction. Initial responses to the faculty and staff survey led to the development of Penn State's series of Excellence in Leadership and Management certificate programs, with individual programs tailored to the needs of administrative assistants, first-line supervisors, managers, and academic department heads.

COLLABORATING THROUGH TEAMWORK

In CQI, a team brings varied experiences and diverse perspectives to the table. Teams share responsibility for a common goal and make decisions collaboratively. This leads to a quality decision and increased acceptance of the changes.

For example, in designated courses, quality teams of students might create a partnership between students and faculty. The students take the responsibility for developing survey questions, collecting

Streamlining Processes at Penn State

Continuous Quality Improvement (CQI) focuses on streamlining processes, saving time and resources, while still providing a quality product or service. Penn State's university-wide CQI initiative began in the fall of 1991, driven by a belief among top-level administrators that there were too many layers of bureaucracy in the university, and that it took too long to get things done. Students were waiting in line in places such as college advising centers, the Bursar's Office, the pharmacy, the library, and computer labs. Initiatives throughout the university eliminated redundancies, reduced steps, and used technology to improve processes in many ways that made life better for students.

eLion, a Web-based interactive system, was initially developed in 1994 and is continuously enhanced and expanded. eLion delivers secure Web-based services to students, academic advisers, faculty, and prospective students, saving them time and giving them 24/7 access to information. Now, each day, eLion processes thousands of transactions, such as transcript and degree audits, adviser communications, changes of major, and student aid and tuition payments.

The pharmacy at University Health Services fills hundreds of prescriptions a day, many of these for students. In the past, turnaround time was too long. The pharmacy staff implemented an automated, robotic system to do the manual work of placing medication in bottles and preparing labels. Staff verifies the contents afterward. This change reduced turnaround time, increased the accuracy of prescriptions, and improved customer satisfaction.

---

and summarizing the data, and sharing the results with the faculty member. This allows students to see improved teaching and learning while the course is underway rather than waiting until the end of the semester.

To better serve its stakeholders, the Office of Student Aid might be organized for continuous teamwork. The staff could be grouped into teams that improve services for students, ensure compliance with federal and state regulations, and improve interoffice communication.

To acknowledge the work of teams, and more effectively share their accomplishments, Penn State recognizes teamwork annually and maintains a database of projects. By 2008, almost 800 teams had worked on improvement and innovation projects across Penn State's many campuses.

Improvement and innovation can be initiated across an entire institution—in academic programs, cocurricular activities, and student and administrative services. These efforts increase the value of the education that students receive and create a student-centered environment.

THE RELATIONSHIP BETWEEN CONTINUOUS IMPROVEMENT AND STRATEGIC PLANNING

What role does continuous improvement (CI) play in strategic planning? Both CI and planning are organizational learning processes. They share the principles of data-driven decision making, broad communication across the organization, assessment of the needs of multiple stakeholders, benchmarking, and strong leadership commitment. Both require critical thinking and attempt to transfer the rigor of learning in the classroom to the larger organization.

George Keller, an educational writer, editor, and planner, said that in the 21st century higher education leaders will be responsible primarily for three things: managing change, financial controls, and quality of service. Leaders will manage new administrative configurations, changes in tenure, networks of colleges linked through technology, three-year baccalaureates, different departmental structures, and interdisciplinary academic programs. Second, they will devote more time and ingenuity to controlling costs, increasing productivity, finding additional revenues, and evaluating expenditures. The third responsibility, maintaining quality of service, will require administrators to vigilantly watch over the quality of teaching, advising, student services, administrative actions, and campus facilities and equipment as never before. Keller's words are ringing true.

The strategic planning processes in academic and academic support units reflect these new ways of managing change, controlling costs, and improving quality. Continuous Quality Improvement (CQI) tools and processes provide strategies for management of change and a framework for effective strategic planning. When CQI informs the planning process:

- Mission and vision statements are based on the needs of external and internal stakeholders. Faculty, staff, and administrators share common understandings and commitments about what it is they wish to accomplish together for their stakeholders.
- Feedback is regularly solicited from students, faculty, staff, employers, parents, and alumni, and then best opinions and observations are used to improve quality and respond to new conditions.
- Casual, political, and crisis-oriented administration is replaced with information-grounded, strategic innovations.
- Quality improvement efforts focus on the core processes of the institution. Strategic planning identifies which processes and subprocesses must be optimized and CQI improves those processes.
- Close oversight and supervision of daily affairs is delegated by top administrators to vice presidents, directors, and department chairs, who in turn delegate more responsibilities to their staff.
- Teamwork and team decision making is fostered. CQI teams are built on trust and operate from a common understanding of the institution's systems and processes and a shared commitment to ongoing improvement.

In summary, strategic planning and CQI:

- Involve faculty, staff, and students at all levels
- Seek and use data that reflect the needs of all the stakeholders
- Look beyond the immediate day-to-day concerns and to the future
- Address limitations, barriers, and weaknesses as well as strengths in goals and objectives
- Set priorities, so that people know where to focus their efforts

- Show collaboration and integration of resources across units

Strategic planning provides the framework for defining an institution's mission, vision, and goals. Continuous Quality Improvement provides principles and tools for guiding the planning and improvement processes.

LEADING PLANNING, ASSESSMENT, AND IMPROVEMENT

LEADING FOR CONTINUOUS IMPROVEMENT

This chapter outlines the fundamentals of establishing and supporting teams to add value to the department or unit. It provides an overview of the role, responsibilities, and activities of the sponsor of an improvement team or initiative, especially in the initial stages of development and support of the team. It also addresses the roles of the team leader, team members, and facilitator, and provides guidelines and suggestions for implementing solutions and recognizing and documenting accomplishments.

INTRODUCTION

Continuous Quality Improvement (CQI) strengthens an institution's mission. CQI is both a philosophy and a set of guiding principles that represent the foundation of a continuously learning, developing, and improving organization, readily able to adapt to the changing needs of its constituents. The four hallmarks of a successful CQI effort are:

- a focus on service to stakeholders
- study of processes
- decisions based on data
- teamwork

Implementing CQI within an organization requires a significant ongoing effort throughout the organization. Leadership at all levels and within all units of the institution is essential to sustain this effort and realize the many benefits of a long-term commitment to creating a quality culture. CQI is not an end in itself, but a means to develop the organization into a fully integrated system.Data collected in identifying areas for improvement support assessment initiatives and development of strategic plans. Development of a culture for improvement and assessment supports the execution of strategic plans.

CQI uses teamwork to accomplish its improvements. Working through teams brings a shared expertise and understanding of systems and a mutual commitment to ongoing improvement. Empowering team members to identify improvements enhances the opportunity for professional development and accomplishment. In the words of one CQI team member, "The greatest aspect of the team was working with many different people from other backgrounds: the multicultural and multidisciplinary nature of the team."

But teams require leadership and support. As Peter Scholtes says in *Teams in the Age of Systems*, "It's not hard to establish a lot of teams, just as it's not hard to plant a lot of seeds in a garden. The hard work of gardening and setting up teams is tending to them, nurturing them, supporting them, and preparing to process what they produce. Such direction, focus, challenge, support, and caretaking must come from leaders. It's part of the leader's new job."

Leading teams is an ongoing process requiring effort, commitment, and resources. However, it is an investment that can provide returns to both the department or unit and the individuals involved.

SPONSORING AN IMPROVEMENT TEAM OR INITIATIVE

Serving as the sponsor of an improvement team or initiative provides an opportunity to move into a coaching role to facilitate the growth of the unit and the professional development of the team members. Developing and implementing improvements, using Penn State's IMPROVE model or another model, gives a leader and manager the opportunity to find ways to more effectively use all resources—human, financial, information, and physical—while at the same time providing an opportunity for unit members to use and further develop their expertise in job-related functions, problem solving, and interpersonal skills. Implementing CQI allows those providing a service to improve that service when they see opportunities or needs, moving related decision making downward. It also helps them in developing their skills to recognize those opportunities and needs for improvement. Sponsors, administrators, directors, and senior managers provide teams with the guidance needed to achieve successful outcomes as they improve processes. Through this support and guidance, a sponsor can foster collaboration and strengthen people, facilitating long-term development of the organization as well as shorter-term process improvement.

The process a team seeks to improve may be identified by the sponsor, by a team member, or by another stakeholder. The team sponsor manages and allocates the resources involved in the process to be improved, and is the one with the authority to implement team solutions. A sponsor's activities fall into four major phases or stages:

- initiating the improvement of a process
- supporting the team
- implementing the team's solutions
- recognizing the team's accomplishments

Responsibilities of a sponsor may include:

- identification of critical processes and review of evaluation criteria
- identification of team members (often with the team leader)
- guiding the team to determine whether incremental improvement or reengineering should be considered
- defining constraints and available resources for the team
- communicating regularly with the team leader
- providing support and information to team members
- removing constraints and barriers to team efforts
- signing off at each step of the process or providing the team with additional guidance to reach sign off
- reviewing solutions from the team
- implementing solutions
- recognizing the team's accomplishments

INITIATING IMPROVEMENT OF A PROCESS

In the first phase, initiating the improvement of a process, actions of the sponsor include:

- identifying critical processes in the unit
- selecting a team leader
- identifying a team facilitator
- selecting team members (possibly with input from the team leader)
- issuing a charter/charge to the team
- defining parameters/criteria/constraints/limitations for the team's work

While there is no required order for completing these actions, generally the first stage will involve identifying a critical process to be improved, and determining whether a team would be an effective way to approach the improvement effort. Clarification of the charge, of criteria for the improvement, of constraints on the process, and identification of all team members may involve collaboration among the sponsor, team leader, team members, and team facilitator.

Identifying a Critical Process

As the one responsible for managing resources—funding, facilities, and personnel—a sponsor makes a significant commitment to the improvement process and wants to ensure that this investment is worthwhile. One way to do this is to focus on improving critical processes—those that are key to the mission, products, or services of the unit. What processes relate directly to customer or constituent needs, service, and satisfaction? The issue for analysis and improvement needs to be carefully selected. Considerations include:

- organizational values
- all stakeholders (their needs and requirements)
- unit vision
    - stretch goals and breakthrough items
    - alignment with organizational mission, vision, and goals

- unit key processes
    - available process data
    - possible evaluation criteria
    - fit within the organizational system
- scope of the process—is it manageable?

Especially for the first improvement initiative in a unit, it is important that the effort have a high probability of success and be able to be completed in a relatively short time (four to six months).

When to Use Teams

Before a team is charged to work on a critical process, it is useful to consider whether a team is the most effective way to address the issue. Teams are not always the answer, and, yes, there may be situations where it is better to use a working group, or no team at all. Teams should not be used for tasks that are simple or obvious, require the input of only one person or a group of individuals, or when a desired solution is in mind. It is appropriate to use teams to address complex tasks, those that exceed the ability of any one individual, or those that require contributions involving a variety of skills, knowledge areas, or perspective.

Peter Scholtes, in *Teams in the Age of Systems*, provides a list of questions to consider when planning to establish and charge a team:

- Is the issue simple or complex? (Complex issues often require teamwork and input from multiple perspectives.)
- Does the issue require a specific area of expertise or several experts from multiple disciplines? (The need for multiple areas of expertise warrants the use of a team.)
- Can it be completed quickly or will it take a longer time? (A team with more members will provide more continuity and "team memory" over time.)
- Does the issue involve a single function or is it cross-functional? (The team should reflect all functional areas if the process crosses functions.)

- Is the issue controversial? (Include potential dissenters on the team to address their concerns and increase the likelihood of their supporting the team's actions.)
- Will the implementation be easy or complex? (Implementers will have a better understanding of the change and the reasoning behind it if they are part of the team developing the solutions.)

Using teams can also support the professional development of team members. As R. Roosevelt Thomas, Jr. points out in *Redefining Diversity*, as an organization becomes more diverse and more complex, working in teams is one way to develop the new skills individuals need to contribute most effectively to the changing organization.

Selecting the Team Leader

Since team members come together to share their expertise and knowledge of the process under consideration, the team leader's role is to function primarily as a coordinator, not a decision maker. However, the team leader should be familiar with the process, and its stakeholders. He or she should be able to draw information from all team members throughout the improvement process, manage scheduling and record keeping within the team, and maintain communications and a working relationship with the sponsor(s). The team leader may also play a key role in selecting the other members of the team. The team leader's role includes:

- serving as the primary communication link between the sponsor and the team
- coordinating team logistics
- planning and evaluating team meetings with the team facilitator
- keeping official records of team activities
- providing access to any information the team needs regarding process improvement
- bridging to each next step in the improvement process

If the team leader supervises team members in their normal work activities, he or she needs to put that role aside during the team activities to allow for open communication without fear of reprisal.

Identifying the Team Facilitator

The team facilitator works with the team and guides them through the improvement process while at the same time maintaining a neutral position regarding the team's specific recommendations. The team facilitator:

- assists the team leader in planning team activities and evaluating team meetings
- coaches the team in use of the improvement model and appropriate analytical tools
- facilitates productive group dynamics
- brings in outside advisers as necessary
- serves as a neutral third party to maintain the team's focus

Selecting the Team Members

The team should be composed of those people who are most familiar with the process being improved, and willing to invest time and energy in improvement efforts. Team members should be ready, willing, and able to:

- participate fully in team meetings
- complete assignments in preparation for team meetings
- make decisions based on facts and data
- maintain an open mind when considering alternatives for process improvements
- commit to the philosophy of process improvement
- follow the ground rules set by the team

In selecting those who will be on the team, look for those who are:

- involved in the process being addressed
- committed to the process
- interdependent on each other
- interested in improvement
- motivated to be on the team

- knowledgable about the process
- and who, as a team, are involved with the entire process from beginning to end

Chartering/Charging the Team

The team charter or charge is a brief document that defines the team's task for all involved, and provides additional information on limits and resources available. The sponsor may want to develop the charter with the team and team leader, with input from key stakeholders, to ensure that all agree on the issue, responsibilities, authority, and timeframe.

Items to address in the charter include:

- identification and clear definition of the process to be studied
- identification of the team sponsor, team leader, and team members
- general expectations for team results (e.g., recommendations, a streamlined process, measurable improvements in the process)
- resource constraints for the team's work
- time constraints for the team's work, and expected completion date
- planned communications between the sponsor and the team

As Peter Scholtes points out in *Teams in the Age of Systems*, no team is entirely autonomous or entirely advisory; but both the team and the sponsor should be clear where these lines are drawn. Lack of regular communication between sponsor and team can lead to unrecognized divergence from expected final products, and wasted resources in final recommendations which cannot be implemented.

Cross-Unit Teams

If the team is a cross-functional or cross-unit team, there will be additional upfront activities to lay the groundwork, identify multiple sponsors, and reach agreement on shared objectives, outcomes, and constraints. Multiple sponsors with differing expectations, unclear charges, or unstated constraints can lead to frustrated, unproductive teams.

Constraints

Most sponsors impose some limitations or boundaries on the solutions or recommendations the teams can suggest. A team needs to be told at the beginning of the improvement process of any constraints or limitations related to:

- funding
- hiring
- time
- space and facilities
- sensitive issues and areas
- possible solutions that the sponsor views as not realistic

And the team needs to be kept up to date about changes in these areas which occur while they are working.

Time is a key factor in continuous improvement, and needs to be addressed very deliberately at the start of the improvement process. Teamwork takes time, and both the sponsor and the team members need to recognize and acknowledge this. Team members need to understand and be assured that the time they spend working on team-related improvement efforts, whether in team meetings or outside of the meetings, is valued, and is as important as their "regular" work. Their success will be measured not in how quickly they can identify improvements, but in the quality of the solutions.

Initial Team Training

The amount and type of training the team needs, and how it is scheduled, will be determined by the experience of the team leader and team members, complexity of the issue, and projected time to complete the project. Team training for all members of the team can ensure clarity about roles, responsibilities, and the team charter, and familiarity with the improvement approach. Training can be incorporated into the team's first meetings. Having sponsor(s) attend at least part of the team training allows for clear communication and demonstrates support for the team.

SUPPORTING THE TEAM

While sponsors do not attend regular team meetings, they do play a critical role in supporting the team. The sponsor should continually ask him or herself: "What can I do to maximize my support for the team as they develop and work?"

As the team progresses through a structured approach, a sponsor's primary tasks are: 1) to sign off on each step, as the team reports findings and plans the next step; or 2) to provide them with additional guidance when the sponsor cannot sign off on a step. The key role is to provide coaching and counseling, support, and encouragement to ensure that the team's work is an effective use of resources—time, personnel, and funds. It is important to communicate regularly with the team leader about the team's progress. The teams are exploring new ground, broadening their perspective as they learn from each other's expertise, and developing solutions that fit within the parameters provided. Through regular communications with the team leader, the sponsor can provide additional information and support in a timely manner.

Team Development

The four stages of group development—form, storm, norm, perform (Tuckman 1965)—are well known. Once a team is formed, it progresses through these stages, albeit at its own pace. If development progresses smoothly, members grow from a group with multiple individual agendas to a team with shared goals and identity. Part of the role of the sponsor is to monitor the group's progress in development as a team, and provide assistance when progress is not smooth.

How can a sponsor nurture a group so that it develops into a fully functioning team? James Kouzes and Barry Posner, in *The Leadership Challenge,* suggest several guidelines.

Foster collaboration—promote cooperative goals and build trust among all involved.

- Use "we" rather than "I."
- Increase interpersonal interactions within your unit and with other units.
- Focus on gains, not losses.
- Include others in planning and problem solving.
- Go first—set the example and take risks.

Strengthen people—give power away, provide choice to those enabled, provide them a means to develop their competence, assign them significant responsibilities, and offer them visible support.

- Move decision making to the lowest level possible.
- Make sure delegated tasks are relevant.
- Train and educate.
- Share information.
- Assist followers in networking.
- Publicize followers' accomplishments.

In addition, the sponsor should be consistent in actions and words, making sure that daily actions provide the team the support they need.

- Monitor the team's progress.
- Communicate with the team leader on a regular basis.
- Act as consultant/coach—help resolve problems that may be slowing the team.
- Motivate and encourage the team.
- Protect the team's time.
- Track the team's paperwork.
- Sign off on status reports and feedback in a timely manner.
- Provide guidance in prioritizing possible solutions.
- Provide the team with access to information and personnel to research their issue.

- Keep the team leader informed about changes in management direction or available resources.
- Approve additions and deletions to the team membership as they are requested by the team.
- Discuss results of each step in the improvement model with the team leader; if unable to sign off, explain the reason, clarify what is necessary to achieve sign off, look for win-win, collaborative resolution of each issue.

IMPLEMENTING TEAM SOLUTIONS

As the sponsor and the team develop a plan to translate recommendations into actions, implementing solutions may be the most difficult step. It's important to remember that this step represents another occasion to enable others and provide them an opportunity for growth and development. The team has a hands-on chance to learn about the planning process—identifying action items, individuals responsible for completing them, and target dates for accomplishment. Actions at this stage include:

- reviewing the team's final report
- implementing all approved solutions in a timely manner
- calling the team back together if problems in implementation occur (if the original team is not the group implementing the solutions)
- identifying future improvement opportunities

Team Report

The team report is an important way to document team accomplishments and share results so that others may benefit. It briefly describes the process under study, identifies the customer(s) and customer concerns, presents the issue statement, lists tools used, and describes solutions and implementation plans. Reports are tailored to the specifics of each team and the process improved, but key elements include:

- identifying information: college or unit sponsoring the team, team name, names of team sponsor, leader, members, and facilitator, when the team was formed

---

Lessons Learned at Penn State

- Start small with a process that people care about improving.
- Relate process improvement initiatives to the unit's strategic planning goals.
- Be patient—the first team will need time to learn how to work together as a team and learn the CQI tools. Subsequent team efforts will probably take less time.
- Be realistic and clear with the team about constraints. If they operate within the constraints, be prepared and willing to implement their solutions.
- Communicate—teams with multiple sponsors can be dysfunctional if sponsors don't communicate regularly and haven't reached agreement on goals and outcomes.
- Don't underestimate the value of a neutral facilitator from outside the unit. Often team leaders, although well intended, are too closely tied to the process to see opportunities for change.
- When choosing a team leader, look for someone who is foremost a good listener and has the ability to keep the playing field level.

- team charge and constraints: the critical process under study, requirements for the solution, job titles or other indicators of the relationship of team members to the critical process
- initial research: identification of the customer and summary of the customer needs/satisfaction data gathered
- issue statement written and performance measure(s) identified
- map of the process
- root causes identified
- solutions identified and implementation plans
- tools appropriate to the process and/or approach
- contacts for additional information

RECOGNIZING TEAM ACCOMPLISHMENTS

Finally, it is important to recognize the team for their accomplishments. While completion of the improvement process will in all likelihood give the team a sense of satisfaction, sharing their results publicly will reinforce the significance. Some of the ways the team can be recognized are:

- publicly acknowledge the team's accomplishments in staff meetings, newsletters, bulletin boards, or other available vehicles
- share the team's successes both inside and outside the department
- reward the team's efforts through letters of recognition that can be included in performance appraisals, certificates, lunches, or other celebrations

REFERENCES

Burton, Terence T. and John W. Moran. (1995). *The Future Focused Organization.* Englewood Cliffs, NJ: Prentice Hall PTR.

Donnellon, Anne. (1996). *Team Talk.* Boston, MA: Harvard Business School.

Katzenbach, Jon R. and Douglas K. Smith, "The Discipline of Teams," *Harvard Business Review*, March-April 1993, pp. 111-120.

Kouzes, James M. and Barry Z. Posner. (1995). *The Leadership Challenge.* San Francisco, CA: Jossey-Bass.

Maddux, Robert B. (1992). *Team Building: An Exercise in Leadership.* Menlo Park CA: Crisp Publications, Inc.

Parker, Glenn M.. (1994). *Cross-Functional Teams.* San Francisco, CA: Jossey-Bass.

Pokras, Sandy. (1995). *Rapid Team Deployment: Building High-Performance Project Teams.* Menlo Park, CA: Crisp Publications, Inc.

Rees, Fran. (1991). *How to Lead Work Teams: Facilitation Skills.* San Diego, CA: Pfeiffer and Company.

Schein, Edgar H. (1985). *Organizational Culture and Leadership.* San Francisco, CA: Jossey-Bass.

Scholtes, Peter R., "Teams in the Age of Systems," *Quality Progress*, December 1995, pp. 51-59.

Thomas, R. Roosevelt, Jr. (1996). *Redefining Diversity.* New York, NY: American Management Association.

Tuckman, Bruce, "Development Sequence in Small Groups," *Psychological Bulletin*, 1965.

ASSESSING FOR IMPROVEMENT

How do faculty and staff work to ensure that students have successful academic experiences? Many faculty and staff assess student learning and co-curricular outcomes, but approaches are suited to the individual unit. For example, an Engineering Science faculty might use student portfolios, the Office of Student Affairs may conduct student satisfaction surveys, and the Master of Health Administration program may survey graduates.

This chapter discusses steps in the assessment process and outlines one approach for implementing an assessment process. Using this approach, faculty and staff can obtain useful, valid, and comprehensive information on student learning outcomes. And, more importantly, assessment results can help improve the quality of teaching, learning, and service to students.

WHAT IS ASSESSMENT?

Assessment is:

"... gathering and evaluating quantitative and/or qualitative information that demonstrates congruence between the institution's mission, goals, and objectives and the actual outcomes of its educational activities." (MSCHE, 2002, p.50)

"... the gathering of information concerning the functioning of students, staff, and institutions of higher education. The information may or may not be in numerical form, but the basic motive for gathering it is to improve the functioning of the institution and its people." (Astin, 1993, p.2)

"... an ongoing process aimed at understanding and improving student learning. It involves making our expectations explicit and public; setting appropriate criteria and high standards for learning quality; systematically gathering, analyzing, and interpreting evidence to determine how well performance matches those expectations and standards; and using the resulting information to document, explain, and improve performance." (Angelo, 1995, p.7)

"... the systematic collection, review, and use of information about educational programs undertaken for the purpose of improving student learning and development." (Palomba and Banta, 1999, p.4)

As these definitions suggest, assessment and quality improvement go hand in hand. Assessment enables faculty and staff to make informed decisions to improve teaching and learning based on whether:

- students receive high-quality instruction in the classroom;
- academic programs provide students with the skills and experiences to meet their future goals; and
- support services ensure the ability of students to succeed academically.

DIMENSIONS OF ASSESSMENT

Assessment occurs throughout an institution. It is found in classrooms, programs, departments, offices and colleges, and ultimately at the institutional level. Assessment can occur in any timeframe: some assessments occur quickly, as when students complete a one-minute assessment of what they have learned in class, while other activities may be lengthier, such as periodic surveys of alumni or accreditation reviews that take months to complete. Assessment happens both within and outside of the institution. Internal assessment includes such areas as 1) formal and informal assessments of teaching and learning in the classroom, including for example, written tests, review of portfolios, and informal feedback mechanisms, 2) review of data reports on such outcomes as grade point averages, retention rates, and graduation rates, and 3) analysis of survey data from classroom or institution-wide surveys. Examples of external data assessment include 1) peer reviews, 2) licensure and certification testing results, and 3) external accreditation in specific disciplines.

The goal of assessment is to improve the quality of teaching, learning, and support services. Without improvement at its core, assessment activities stagnate.

Another institutional goal is to be accountable. Students, parents, alumni, accrediting agencies, and the federal government all expect the institution to provide some evidence that students are learning and progressing through their educations.

As faculty, administrators, and staff work to implement assessment, both improvement and accountability are achievable. Assessing for the sake of simply meeting institutional, departmental, or external mandates misses the critical linkage between appraisal of teaching and learning methods and the chance to make these outcomes better.

IMPLEMENTING ASSESSMENT

In their handbook on assessment, Palomba and Banta (1999) lay out six essential strategies for implementing an assessment process:

1. Agree on goals and objectives.
2. Design and implement a thoughtful assessment process.
3. Involve individuals from on and off campus.
4. Select or design and implement data collection approaches.
5. Examine, share, and act on assessment findings.
6. Regularly reexamine the assessment process.

Generally, a small group of persons will carry out these six steps, based on the input and involvement of a much larger group of stakeholders.

"As educators, we have a responsibility to the publics that support or depend on us to provide information about the ways in which our students meet goals and expectations. But that responsibility goes beyond the reporting of such information; our deeper obligation—to ourselves, our students, and society—is to improve." (AAHE, 1996)

1. Agree on Goals and Objectives

As a first step, it is essential that any group working on assessment identify goals and objectives for the teaching and learning processes or any other process. For teaching and learning, the question to be addressed is "What should students be able to do and what should they know?" In other areas, the purpose and intent of the services provided must be identified and goals and objectives set accordingly. Well developed goals are stated clearly, are measurable, and are actionable.

Many academic programs may already have defined learning goals and objectives for students. Programs with established student learning goals and objectives can use these as the basis of assessment. For those programs without established goals, Palomba and Banta recommend that faculty apply Bloom's (1956) taxonomy of cognitive objectives when identifying and developing goals for student learning. These are knowledge, comprehension, application, analysis, synthesis, and evaluation—all well-established foundations in the teaching/learning community.

Building on these, the Middle States Commission suggests that assessment of student learning "might incorporate such outcomes as cumulative learning, analytical and information skills, specific competencies, knowledge and cognitive abilities, student attitude development and growth, life skills, student activity involvement, and physical skills and techniques." (MSCHE, 2002, p. 52)

These skills and competencies start in the classroom, but the interaction between individual courses and program structure also affects student outcomes. Assessment may include indicators of academic success like retention, graduation, and satisfaction. Course and departmental goals likely will be more specific than institution-wide goals.

The number of goals and objectives set should be manageable, especially since most of them will have multiple measures. In addition, goals should be "most important, widely accepted by the various stakeholders, meaningful, sufficiently explicit, and interconnected among the various academic levels and curricula within the institution." (MSCHE, 2003, p.18)

Some steps to take in developing goals and objectives are:

- Inventory current program or department learning or other objectives.
- Review current course syllabi for learning objectives.
- Review Bloom's taxonomy of cognitive objectives for learning outcomes.
- Complete the Teaching Goals Inventory from the MSCHE (2003, pp. 23-26).
- Identify what the "ideal" completer of the course or program would look like and set goals and objectives based on this.

2. Design and Implement a Thoughtful Approach to Assessment Planning

Assessment occurs at many levels and for many reasons in most higher education institutions. As a second step in the process, Palomba and Banta suggest that in planning assessment, faculty, staff, and administrators must determine the approach to, and nature of, the assessment.

One dimension to consider is the application of the results. Some assessment activities are formative while others are summative. Formative assessment, as defined by Leskes (2002), is "the gathering of information about student learning—during the progression of a course or program and usually repeatedly—to improve the learning of those students." Thus, testing in a classroom throughout a semester typically provides feedback to faculty and students on an ongoing basis and facilitates immediate improvement. The diagnostic nature of formative assessment highlights specific areas that are lacking. Summative assessment is "the gathering of information at the conclusion of a course, program, or undergraduate career to improve learning or to meet accountability demands." (Leskes, 2002) It typically provides data for monitoring program performance and to provide accountability. Although it may not impact current students, summative assessment affects individual students since the results are applicable to future cohorts of students.

Thinking about how the results will be used after they are collected may help in developing specific strategies and methods. For example, results may be used to improve instruction, to initiate curriculum discussion among faculty, to implement revision as necessary, or to provide data for reporting to outside accrediting agencies.

For assessment to be successful, it should result in useful, applicable results and the methodology used to collect assessment data should provide valid and reliable measures. Valid indicators measure the dimension they intend to measure, while reliable ones ensure consistent measurement when assessing the same dimension.

This second step results in a plan for assessment that describes the overall nature of the assessment. Factors to consider are:

- Where will the assessment take place? Will it occur in the classroom? From standardized tests given outside the classroom? From surveys at the institutional level?
- When will it occur? Will the assessment occur each semester? Every year? Another time period?
- Who will be assessed? Will all students be included, as occurs in classroom testing, or will a sample be used, as for alumni surveys?
- Who will conduct the assessment? What specific responsibilities should be assigned?
- How will the results be used for improvement?

3. Involve Individuals from On and Off Campus

Involving numerous stakeholders improves assessment. Inclusion helps to ensure that the design of assessment represents the needs of these groups. Important stakeholders are students, faculty, staff, alumni, and employers, but depending on the type of program or service being assessed, there may be others like community members or accrediting agency representatives. Identifying all parties involved in teaching and learning and other processes will help in developing a well-rounded and inclusive approach to assessment and identify areas for improvement that might otherwise be missed.

In a 2004 survey of academic and department heads at Penn State, 75 percent agreed that "Examination of assessment data leads to decisions about our academic program."

---

4. Select or Design and Implement Data Collection Approaches

There are two basic ways to collect data. One is a direct approach in which students display their knowledge through testing or essays, while the other is an indirect approach. Direct approaches include such methods as student portfolios, capstone courses, standardized tests, and in-class tests. Indirect measures may include student retention rates, alumni satisfaction levels, and graduate employment indicators.

When developing data collection methodologies for assessment, it is important to keep the process as simple as possible. However, it is also vital that the assessment include multiple measures because teaching and learning are complex processes. Both short- and long-term indicators should be considered to account for the complexity of the processes and to address the needs of multiple stakeholders. Assessment may include both quantitative and qualitative indicators to address multifaceted levels.

In developing a data collection process for assessment, some steps inclued the following:

- Identify the current sources of data that are available for assessment
- Determine whether new instruments need to be developed or whether current instruments meet assessment needs
- Study the assessment plans and methodologies of other universities and colleges
- Review handbooks of assessment if new methodologies are necessary (see listing at end of this document)

5. Examine, Share, and Act on Assessment Findings

As groups working on the assessment activities complete their work, they may want to share the results with others within and outside of the institution by providing summaries of the results and recommendations for improvements.

"Assessment is a process whose power is cumulative. Though isolated, "one-shot" assessment can be better than none, [and] improvement is best fostered when assessment entails a linked series of activities undertaken over time. " (AAHE, 1996)

Once assessment results are available, the measured outcomes should be compared with the expected outcomes. If they are not aligned, recommendations from the findings can address specific steps to improve the outcomes. For example, recommendations could relate to changing existing course content, modifying teaching methods, adding new courses, or sequencing courses differently.

Rather than occurring sporadically, assessment should occur on a regular basis. A systematic approach to assessment helps in refining assessment measures, results in better measures, and provides comparative data for improvement purposes.

A report that presents the results and a process to share the results are the final products of this step. Factors to consider in the development of both include:

- Identify the gaps between the measured outcomes and the expected outcomes. These gaps are the areas on which to focus.
- Present assessment results in a clear, easy to understand manner.
- Determine the stakeholders who will receive the information.
- Identify how stakeholder suggestions and recommendations will be collected, considered, and incorporated into course, program, or service improvements.

6. Regularly Reexamine the Assessment Process

Regular review of the assessment process will confirm that the results are valid and reliable, and that they are meeting the needs of the community, including stakeholders. If assessment findings are not meeting the needs, the process may need to be revised.

As with any Continuous Quality Improvement effort, people closest to the process are most knowledgeable about it and should be the ones to review the process. Changes to the process and the reasons for the changes should be documented. As Suskie (2004) points out, "All the time and effort that goes into assessment is worthwhile only if that work eventually leads to improved teaching and learning." (p. 300) Suskie recommends several areas to examine, including whether the assessment met the expectations, if the quality of the assessment results was acceptable, what the costs and benefits were, and possible modifications to the process.

A thoughtful review of the process used for assessment can lead to improvements in efficiency of the process, accuracy of the findings, and usability of the results, and ultimately result in an enhanced living/learning community for students.

SELECTED RESOURCES FOR ASSESSMENT

Web Sites

Internet Resources for Higher Education Outcomes Assessment (http://www2.acs.ncsu.edu/UPA/assmt/ resource.htm)

Middle States Commission on Higher Education, Best Practices in Outcomes Assessment (http://www.msche.org/publications/BESTOA050208135229.pdf)

Practical Assessment, Research and Evaluation (http://PAREonline.net)

References

American Association of Higher Education. (1996). 9 principles of good practice for assessing student learning. Cited in http://ultibase.rmit.edu.au/Archives/ articles.htm#june97.

Angelo, Thomas. (1995). "Reassessing (and defining) assessment". *AAHE Bulletin*. 48(3): 7-9.

Astin, Alexander. (1993). *Assessment for Excellence: The philosophy and practice of assessment and evaluation in higher education*. Phoenix, AZ: Oryx Press.

Leskes, Andrea. (2002). "Beyond confusion: An assessment glossary". *Peer Review* 4 (2/3):42-43.

Middle States Commission on Higher Education. (2002). ***Characteristics of Excellence in Higher Education: Eligibility Requirements and Standards of Accreditation***. Philadelphia, PA: Middle States Commission on Higher Education.

Middle States Commission on Higher Education. (2003). *Student Learning Assessment: Options and Resources*. Philadelphia, PA: Middle States Commission on Higher Education.

Palomba, Catherine A. and Trudy W. Banta. (1999). *Assessment Essentials: Planning, Implementing, and Improving Assessment in Higher Education*. San Francisco, CA: Jossey-Bass Publishers.

Suskie, Linda. (2004). *Assessing Student Learning: A Common Sense Guide*. Bolton, MA: Anker Publishing Company, Inc.

LEADING A SUCCESSFUL INNOVATION INITIATIVE

WHAT DOES IT TAKE TO MAKE AN INNOVATION OR IMPROVEMENT INITIATIVE SUCCESSFUL?

Over the past year, 26 groups in Mastering SuperVision have been answering this question as part of the Leading Improvement in Your Workgroup module provided by Penn State's Office of Planning and Institutional Assessment. Their answers may surprise you—for their simplicity, straightforwardness, and obviousness. We share their thoughts as a quick guide in reviewing how innovation, improvement, and goal accomplishment can be supported in a higher education environment.

OBSERVATIONS FROM MASTERING SUPERVISION

Many of the groups identified similar categories of behavior to lead innovation, although there is variation in what they named the categories (and over 50 categories were named). We have clustered some of these categories and behaviors to emphasize the similarities and patterns and to focus on the most frequently identified categories.

Overall, the groups recognized *communication* most often as a key category. Some of the specific behaviors under the category of communication included listening to others, gathering input, respect for all, and clear expectations. Some other frequently cited categories of behaviors included encouragement/open-mindedness, leadership/attitude, goals/needs, feedback/process assessment, and teamwork. Some specific behaviors mentioned for *encouragement/open-mindedness* included consensus building, having an open-door policy, openness to feedback, and showing confidence in others. *Leadership/attitude* behaviors included being fair and honest, flexible, and able to delegate. Setting clear goals and creative thinking were included in *goals/needs*. *Feedback/process assessment* behaviors included follow through and recognition of positive steps. *Teamwork* behaviors included cooperation on complex tasks and being a team member, not just a teacher. Figure 7.1 provides additional specific behaviors for these key categories.

It's important to point out the interrelationships of each of these categories. Teamwork requires clear communication, obtaining input from others, seeking feedback, and consensus building. Data and goals are needed to help teams identify and address problems and solutions.

It's also important to point out the difficulty of categorizing these interrelated behaviors. In many cases, when the lists from different groups were compared, the same or similar behaviors had been placed in different key categories (respect is part of both communication and encouragement, for example). Finally, while not categorized in exactly the same format, the groups generally identified behaviors that fit this book's definition of Continuous Quality Improvement—a people-based management system that seeks to continually improve performance and exceed customer expectations by using data to improve key processes—and its four components: teams, stakeholders, data, and processes.

KEY LEADERSHIP QUALITIES FROM RECENT LITERATURE

At the fall 2005 Mastering SuperVision graduation ceremony, guest speaker Nancy Eaton, dean of the university libraries at Penn State, shared the six most important leadership qualities identified by Bill Creech in *The Five Pillars of TQM: How to Make Total Quality Management Work for You* (Truman Talley Books/ Dutton, 1994). They are:

1. Courage: In dealing with others, in sticking to principles, and in being willing to change your mind or admit that you don't know and need to find out.

Figure 7.1: Some Key Behaviors for Successful Innovation

Communication	Encouragement/Open-Mindedness
• Active listening • Better communication among coworkers • Clear direction • Clear expectations • Communicate information that is important to others • Communicate success when innovations work • Gather the input of others • Respect to all voices at the table	• Let others be creative • Reward success • Show confidence in ability of employee • Show enthusiasm • Consensus building • Open door and E-mail and personal contact • Respect for others' ideas • Appreciation, openness to feedback • Encourage everyone's input • Support professional development
Leadership/Attitude	**Feedback/Process Assessment**
• Lead by example • Flexibility in adapting to different personalities • Team builder • Dependable • Trusting • Fair • Positive attitude • Coaching • Ability to delegate • Initiative • Risk taking • Honesty	• Follow through • Provide feedback • Customer-centered actions • Find and try new tools to reduce labor intensive processes • Recognition of positive steps • Streamlining processes • Question processes • Discuss anticipated challenges and changes • Reflection/evaluation of current processes • Actively look for ways to improve • Seek data
Goals/Needs	**Teamwork**
• Define individual goals • Set clear goals for unit (strategic plan) • Creative thinking/Not "how do we do it now," but "how do we want to do it" • Commitment to customer satisfaction • Aware of the "big picture"—where the unit is heading	• Cooperation on complex tasks • Team oriented • Promote teamwork • Facilitate team oriented problem solving • Be a team member and not just a teacher

2. Confidence: Believing that you can do it, without being arrogant, recognizing the need to keep growing and learning, not being threatened by change.
3. Savvy: Understanding reality as well as theory, recognizing what you don't know.
4. Maturity: Making reasoned decisions, respecting the dignity of all.
5. Integrity: Being honest, willing to give or receive bad news, sharing information.
6. Desire: Leading to make life better for others and help the organization succeed.

Peter Drucker defined innovation as "change that creates a new dimension of performance." *Leading for Innovation and Organizing for Results*, published by the Drucker Foundation (2002), brings together the thoughts of 23 contributors. Some of the common themes in the essays address the importance of an organizational culture that encourages and supports innovation, a leader who lives and demonstrates the organizational values and culture, and an atmosphere that allows for risk taking and testing and tolerates failure. Howard Gardner and Kim Barberich address the importance of values and ethical behaviors on the part of the leader, specifically a sense of responsibility, honesty and accountability, faith in the organization, and the belief in their contribution to a common good. Robert Knowling emphasizes the importance of a clear vision and strategy, and measures that help people focus their efforts. In our age of rapid technological change, James Burke looks at leaders as facilitators and mentors rather than providers of answers and solutions.

In *Continuous Quality Improvement in Higher Education* (American Council on Education/Praeger Series on Higher Education, 2004), John Dew and Molly Nearing address the components of successful leadership for improvement and innovation in a university environment. First, expanding on earlier models of leadership styles, they recognize the continuum of faculty and staff involvement in decision making, ranging from low, in which the leader decides and announces a decision, to high, in which decision making is delegated to the group. They add to the traditional model the outcome of a leader making no decision, which can lead to chaos, and also recognize that, with low involvement in decision making, the group may ignore the decision. Second, Dew and Nearing address the importance in an academic environment of knowing in advance what process will be used to reach a decision, and ensuring that there is consensus regarding this process and agreement that the process is fair and effective. Finally, Dew and Nearing introduce the LUIS model, used at the State University of New York, Binghamton, to reach consensus, in which participants agree that:

- I can Live with this decision
- I Understand this decision
- I was Involved in this decision
- I will Support this decision

APPLYING THESE INSIGHTS

Leading effective innovation requires basic information that most of us already have. Occasional assistance or training may be necessary to learn a specific tool or facilitate a particular event, but most of the time, leaders just need to pay attention to what they are doing, how they are making decisions and dealing with the people around them, and how these basic ideas can be put into practice. We have more knowledge and wisdom than we may realize. We just need to apply it.

ENHANCING TEAMWORK AND COLLABORATION

HOW TO RECOGNIZE A COLLABORATIVE TEAM ENVIRONMENT

Katzenbach and Smith (1999) provide a widely accepted definition of a team: "A team is a small number of people with complementary skills who are committed to a common purpose, performance goals, and approach for which they hold themselves mutually accountable." A collaborative team environment is characterized by values and beliefs that support the principles of continuous quality improvement (CQI). It includes participative decision making, collaboration, and continuous learning. Members share a common vision and respect for one another. Staff are organized and/or organize themselves in formal and informal, temporary, or longer-term teams. This may include work teams, problem solving teams, centers of excellence, research teams, and cross-functional teams.

WHAT ARE THE POTENTIAL BENEFITS?

A collaborative team environment:

- Encourages the participation of staff at all levels of the institution in decision making. The specific knowledge that each person brings and the broadened input of a team lead to better decisions. It also heightens morale and enables people to take pride in their work.

- Fosters a focus on customer needs, which increases effectiveness and overall performance.
- Increases efficiency by cutting down steps and eliminating redundancies.
- Supports a positive attitude toward change that can help the institution adjust to future changes in the environment, economy, technology, and market.
- Provides a common language that creates more efficient and effective communication both horizontally and vertically across the institution.
- May reduce costs and improve overall performance in many ways, including faster and more reliable decisions, doing things right the first time, improving customer satisfaction, and eliminating redundancies.

HOW DO WE GET STARTED?

Assessing the current environment within your unit is helpful in building a team-based environment. This can be done using questions such as those in the checklist below. If possible, involve all staff in the assessment. The assessment will give you a baseline measure of your current environment as well as ideas about possible areas for improvement.

Team Effectiveness Checklist

The following checklist has been developed from the Workforce Focus component of the Baldrige National Quality Program Education Criteria for Performance Excellence (National Institute of Standards and Technology, 2007).

In your unit, how do you:

- Assess team capabilities and needs?
- Assess team performance and provide feedback and recognition?

- Foster a culture of:
    - Cooperation
    - Communication
    - Information flow
    - Skill sharing
    - Goal setting
    - Empowerment and initiative
    - Innovation
- Develop new skills and competencies?
- Develop leadership?
- Transfer knowledge from departing faculty or staff?
- Recruit and retain team members?
- Reinforce a focus on students, stakeholders, and the organization?
- Reinforce a focus on achievement of action plans?

REFERENCES

National Institute of Standards and Technology Baldrige National Quality Program. (2007). *Education Criteria for Performance Excellence.* www.quality.nist.gov/.

Bens, I. (1999). *Facilitation at a Glance: A Pocket Guide of Tools and Techniques for Effective Meeting Facilitation.* Cincinnati, OH: Association for Quality and Participation.

Brassard, M. and D. Ritter. (1994). *The Memory Jogger II: A Pocket Guide of Tools for Continuous Improvement & Effective Planning.* Methuen, MA: GOAL/QPC.

Griswold, A. (2000). *Structuring Effective Sponsorship.* Presented at the September 15, 2000 meeting of Penn State's Quality Advocates' Network. University Park, PA.

Katzenbach, J.R. & D.K. Smith. (1999). *The Wisdom of Teams: Creating the High-Performance Organization.* New York: Harper Business.

Scholtes, P.R. (1998). *The Leader's Handbook—Making Things Happen, Getting Things Done.* New York: McGraw-Hill.

Scholtes, P.R., B. Joiner, and B. Streibel. (1996). *The Team Handbook (second edition).* Madison, WI: Joiner Associates.

Senge, P., C. Roberts, R. Ross, B. Smith, and A. Kleiner. (1994). *The Fifth Discipline Fieldbook: Strategies and Tools for Building a Learning Organization.* New York: Doubleday.

Senge, P., A. Kleiner, C. Roberts, R. Ross, G. Roth, B. Smith. (1999). *The Dance of Change: The Challenges to Sustaining Momentum in Learning Organizations*. New York: Doubleday.

One Effective Model: Penn State's Office of Student Aid

The Office of Student Aid at Penn State is organized for continuous teamwork. Staff members are organized into six standing teams and many informal teams. The office's leader, Anna Griswold, places emphasis on the interrelationship of teams. She believes that the team structure has helped staff grapple with constant change, and remain flexible.

Teams improve services for students, ensure compliance with federal and state regulations, and improve interoffice processes to help them work better for staff. Team leaders are expected to practice CQI principles.

"We almost forgot that teams are in operation now," says Griswold. Most teams are informal and use data to review current processes, brainstorm, and identify problems. When more is at stake, they use formal CQI teams. Anyone within the office can identify the need for a team.

Decision making in a team environment

"Staff are involved in most of the decisions in the office," says Griswold. Each team meets every one to two weeks. The team leaders meet once a week with Griswold to anticipate the week's activities and potential concerns.

The importance of communication

"Communication is critical for achieving effective outcomes," says Griswold. Channels of communication in the office support the integration of CQI principles into Student Aid's everyday activity. Griswold encourages each team leader to understand the dynamics of effective communication. The entire office is informed of team progress at weekly meetings and via E-mail. Griswold emphasizes that it's important for her to periodically ask staff how their teamwork is going. Student Aid's teams consult with each other to discover the effects of process changes, and they use flowcharting to ensure that all staff affected by the improvement understand the process changes. Flowcharting is important when a process is changed to give an overview of the impact of a decision or change on other teams.

Leader as coach

In the team-structured environment at Student Aid, Griswold tries to operate primarily in the role of coach. She helps teams when they are at a crossroads—for example, when they need resources or need help dealing with a particularly problematic regulation. She takes care to continually ask, "Why are we doing what we do in the way we do it?" She helps teams follow up to ensure their recommendations are implemented, and makes sure the recommendations are given a "home" within the team structure.

Reinforcing the team environment

At Student Aid, the collaborative team environment is fully integrated into daily work. Griswold's philosophy is, "If 'team' isn't the way we do work, then it's getting in the way of our work... the use of teams is a part of what we do rather than apart from what we do." She creates the climate for the team culture to thrive. She stays in touch with the team's progress so there are no surprises, and she implements all solutions they generate. This action sends the message that she values quality and purposeful change. Staff at Student Aid state that "to see the results of the team implemented is a great reward." Griswold trusts and values the recommendations of those who are doing the work. She feels that it's important to acknowledge team successes, so she makes sure that this happens at least once a month.

The Staff Review and Development Program (SRDP) has been modified for the organizational team structure in the office. Each team works together to assess its progress and accomplishments of the past year and to set team goals for the new year. Each member of the team signs the SRDP. Numerical ratings are not assigned to teams or to individual team members. The development goals for each team support the office-wide strategic plan and goals.

IMPLEMENTING A PLAN

One of the most challenging aspects of planning is implementing the plan—getting what's on paper to come to life and achieving the goals and accomplishments included in the plan. Successful implementation needs to begin when work on the plan begins.

Keep these points in mind while developing the plan:

- **Communicate.** Organizational communication about the plan and the planning process needs to start as soon as work begins to develop the planning process. While you won't be able to share a detailed planning process right at the start, you will be able to let people know the reasons for the plan, how it will be used within the organization, and what the impact of having a longer-term plan will be on the organization.
- **Engage.** Include all or representative groups of constituents within and outside the organization during the planning process. Get their input. There are many ways to do this —face-to-face town meetings or focus groups, surveys, task forces on specific issues or topics, or involvement of a large group in the actual drafting of the plan. The best fit will be determined by the culture and size of the institution.
- **Align.** An effective plan cannot be developed in a vacuum. Be aware of trends in your field, the environment you work

in, and the direction of any larger organization to which your unit might belong. Ensure the resulting strategies and goals of your plan are aligned with higher level goals.

Once the plan is written, you'll need to:

- **Keep it moving.** Get senior leadership visibly behind the plan. Have them share with the whole organization the information they receive in progress reports. Demonstrate that the organization supports implementation of the plan to keep it from becoming a shelf document.
- **Communicate.** Share the plan throughout and outside of the organization. Use multiple formats, adapted to the audience—the Web, brief brochures, and detailed action plans. Update the information to reflect progress and accomplishments.
- **Engage people.** Implementing strategies is a lot of work—it's implementing change. Engaging more people will make it possible to spread the workload. Those people engaged in the implementation will feel ownership for the plan.
- **Set priorities.** All of the goals and strategies in the plan cannot be implemented and accomplished at the same time. Spread activities out over the life of the plan. Review the strategies and determine the best places to start. This may be influenced by opportunities for quick successes, by a logical ordering of strategies that depend on actions completed in earlier strategies, or by an annual cycle of organizational activities. A matrix that shows when each strategy will be started and how long it will take to complete may be a useful attachment to the plan.
- **Have a point person or leader for each goal or initiative.** One designated point of contact for an initiative will make it easier to share information, monitor the status, and coordinate work across all components of the plan.
- **Identify measures.** Measures and clear expectations make it possible to see how you are doing, what progress you've made on a strategy, what successes you have had, and when you have accomplished a goal. But the plan should be data informed, not data driven. Data is a means to an end, not an end in itself.

- **Link the plan to daily activities.** Keep the plan visible by integrating it into regular activities such as staff meetings. Drill down from strategies to show how they are related to daily activities.
- **Set milestones within the plan.** Like project management, develop action plans for individual initiatives within the plan. Determine who is responsible for what, when it will be started and completed, and what intermediate accomplishments are needed to achieve final results. This will help to determine when adjustments need to be made and make progress more apparent.
- **Have an easy way to track and summarize progress.** Being able to recognize even partial accomplishments and progress can be rewarding and motivating. But keep resources focused on implementing the initiatives, not on tracking progress.
- **Recognize accomplishments.** Recognizing what has been done can generate energy to do more. Don't wait until a project or plan is completed to recognize success and celebrate. Recognize past accomplishments and new milestones during the implementation of an initiative.
- **Learn from the past.** Plans are not written in stone. As you implement your plan or initiatives, monitor trends and the environment. Track which approaches work well and which ones need refinement, and adapt as you go.

A lot of time and work go into developing a plan. Include in that time the strategies and activities that will support accomplishing goals.

REFERENCES

"Best Practices in Implementing Strategic Plans," *Quality Advocates*, November 11, 2005 http://www.psu.edu/president/pia/advocates/2005/11/index.htm.

Dooris, Michael J., Kelley, John M., and Trainer, James F., Eds. *Successful Strategic Planning, New Directions in Institutional Research, #123*, Fall 2004.

"Implementing Your Strategic Plan," *Quality Advocates*, October 1, 2008 http://www.psu.edu/president/pia/advocates/2008/10/01/index.html.

"Seven Key Points for Successful Planning," *Quality Endeavors #115*, December 2008 http://www.psu.edu/president/pia/newsletter/news0115.html.

APPROACHES FOR PLANNING, ASSESSMENT, AND IMPROVEMENT

A STRUCTURED APPROACH TO ORGANIZATIONAL IMPROVEMENT

This chapter is based on Penn State's IMPROVE model, a structured approach to facilitate problem solving, decision making, and process improvement teamwork.

The IMPROVE model is an expansion of the Plan-Do-Check-Act model introduced by Walter Shewhart and popularized by W. Edwards Deming. It is an analytical and social process that provides structure for team discussions, which in turn fosters a collaborative climate that builds community within the organization. IMPROVE also fosters constructive discussion of multiple viewpoints, thereby enhancing creativity and innovation. This structured approach to teamwork has helped teams at Penn State to improve and redesign processes, programs, and services. It has facilitated organizational community by making it easier to work together to share ideas through the use of a common framework.

PENN STATE'S IMPROVE MODEL

I Identify and Select Process for Improvement
M Map the Critical Process
P Prepare Analysis of Process Performance
R Research and Develop Possible Solutions
O Organize and Implement Improvements
V Verify and Document Results
E Evaluate and Plan for Continuous Improvement

The IMPROVE model is a problem solving strategy that helps a group of people engage in structured communication to design or redesign a process, solve a problem, and make decisions. Some of the basic concepts related to this model include:

Efficiency and Effectiveness

Efficiency

- Internal performance measure of process operations
- Improvement may benefit process owners as well as customers
- Can be measured using cost or time data
- Doing THINGS RIGHT!

Effectiveness

- External performance measure of output or quality
- Should be measured the way that customers measure it
- Can be measured using attribute or variable data
- Doing the RIGHT THINGS!!

Outputs and outcomes

Outputs = what you do
Outcomes = the impact your outputs have

RELATIONAL ISSUES

Characteristics of teams using the IMPROVE model: Like other problem-solving and decision-making groups, a team using the IMPROVE model goes through an evolutionary process where the decisions emerge over time. Use of the model is circular, rather than linear. This means that a team will go back and forth between the seven stages as appropriate. Part of the facilitator's job is to help the team recognize when it's time to move between the seven stages. Just like other models, a team using the IMPROVE model is influenced by individual-level variables such as communication styles and personal values. The team is also influenced by group climate. The facilitator plays an important role in establishing a group climate of respect and open, balanced communication. The facilitator also models effective task and relational communication roles. The stages of the IMPROVE model lay the groundwork for taking advantage of a group's strengths through the use of tools that encourage a greater diversity of perspectives. Finally, teams are influenced by external forces including organizational goals and values, deadlines, and budget. Paradoxically, the use of a structured communication process has freed teams to work more creatively to solve problems in a wide variety of areas.

THE "I" STAGE—IDENTIFY AND SELECT PROCESS FOR IMPROVEMENT

Goal of the "I" Stage

- To establish a clear scope and purpose for the project

Tools

- Affinity Diagram
- Brainstorming
- Check Sheet
- Is/Is Not Analysis
- Pareto Chart
- Stakeholder Communication: Surveys, Interviews, and Focus Groups

Relational Issues

- Establish a constructive group climate
- Clarify roles, attendance expectations
- Manage meetings effectively
- Establish a shared understanding of the team's purpose

Approach

A process improvement project starts by identifying which processes need to be improved. This is often done by researching the expectations of your customers and determining where their needs are not being met.

A process is defined as a series of steps taken to get the job done. In your work there are many processes that you perform each day. For example, there are processes for handling correspondence, scheduling meetings, making travel arrangements, teaching class, conducting meetings, and doing research.

To start:

- Determine primary stakeholders/constituents
- Identify their needs and expectations
- List processes that fulfill these expectations
- Determine how you can measure the success of these processes

Processes that do not meet the expectations of your customers should be considered for improvement.

The outcome of this analysis should be an issue statement that indicates the specific issue the team intends to address in its improvement efforts. This does not mean that a team should have preconceived solutions, but rather, that they have identified processes and measures of performance.

There are three parts to an issue statement:

Part	**Example**
Process	Billing, travel reimbursement, course registration
Measure	Turnaround time, number of occurrences
Direction	Increase, decrease, eliminate

Some sample issue statements:

- Decrease account closing time
- Increase number of students completing student aid application

A team may start with a more general charge, and may not be able to develop a specific issue statement until baseline information on the current processes and performance data is available.

Early in its work the team should develop its charter—a contract between the team and the individual with authority to implement change. The charter includes what the team is working on (their charge or issue statement), boundaries and resources, and completion date. Typical boundaries or constraints may include:

- No new positions
- No significant amount of money
- No change to the union agreement
- Fit all changes into the new product schedule

THE "M" STAGE—MAP THE PROCESS

Goal of the "M" Stage

- To establish a shared understanding of the current situation

Tools

- Flowchart (traditional and top down)

Relational Issues

- Establish norms for the constructive use of conflict communication and sensitivity to diversity issues
- Create Stakeholder Communication Plan

Approach

Establishing a baseline, a shared understanding of the current situation or process being improved, can be done in words. More often, since a picture can be worth a thousand words, it is done through a flowchart, also known as a process map. Flowcharts can also be used for training and reference material on the job. You may not know all the steps in the process and may need input from others to determine the steps. Talk to others who may be able to help you.

THE "P" STAGE—PREPARE ANALYSIS OF PROCESS PERFORMANCE

Goal of the "P" Stage

- To assess process performance and analyze the cause of problems that are identified

Tools

- Histograms
- Run charts

- Control charts
- Fishbone diagram

Relational Issues

- Reinforce buy in for the use of structured communication tools to encourage critical thinking and avoid premature conclusions

Approach

It is important to measure the current performance of the process that your team is working to improve. In this step you first prepare an analysis of the process to determine how well the process you selected is currently performing. Then you analyze the process to determine the potential causes of performance problems.

First, determine which data to collect. This can be done by identifying what aspects of the process are most important to your stakeholders. Is the quality of the process most important? Affordability? Timeliness? Courtesy of your staff?

Second, gather data on the performance of the aspects that are most important to your stakeholders. For example, if timeliness is important you should measure the time your process currently takes for completion.

Third, after gathering process performance data, analyze the data to determine potential causes and effects of the performance problems.

THE "R" STAGE—RESEARCH AND DEVELOP POSSIBLE SOLUTIONS

Goal of the "R" Stage

- To propose, assess, and prioritize potential solutions

Tools

- Benchmarking
- Criteria Matrix
- Multivoting
- Ranking

Relational Issues

- Reinforce equal participation and focused communication by assessing both the positive and negative aspects of potential solutions

Approach

In this step you research and develop a list of possible solutions or specific changes that will improve the process.

You then select the best combination of solutions, in terms of costs and benefits, to achieve your purpose.

THE "O" STAGE—ORGANIZE AND IMPLEMENT IMPROVEMENTS

Goal of the "O" Stage

- To plan and conduct the implementation of priority solutions

Tools

- Gantt Chart
- PERT Chart
- Responsibility Matrix

Relational Issues

- Address organizational change issues by planning for stakeholder communication and the involvement of stakeholders in the implementation of solutions
- Clarify responsibility for implementation

Approach

In this step you organize and develop a plan to implement your solution. You may want to think of this as project management.

THE "V" STAGE—VERIFY AND DOCUMENT RESULTS

Goal of the "V" Stage

- To assess the effectiveness of solutions

Tools

- Histograms
- Run charts/Control charts
- Stakeholder communication: surveys, focus groups, and interviews

Relational Issues

- Maintain team momentum through the elapsed time needed for implementation

Approach

In this step you verify and document results. Essentially you decide if improvement has in fact occurred. Once that has been established, you need to have a plan for monitoring your success.

THE "E" STAGE—EVALUATE AND PLAN FOR CONTINUOUS IMPROVEMENT

Goal of the "E" Stage

- To share lessons learned and anticipate future improvements

Tools

- Many of the previously listed tools

Relational Issues

- Stakeholder communication
- Encourage closure by celebrating team success

Approach

Sometimes when you improve a process, you discover other opportunities for improvement. In this step, you determine what those opportunities might be and what steps to take. It is critical to continue to analyze and evaluate the performance of the process.

Team members have also gained new skills, and there may be more opportunities for application of those skills.

The opportunities for improvement don't end once your process has been improved. Change is continuous and improvement needs to be continuous as well.

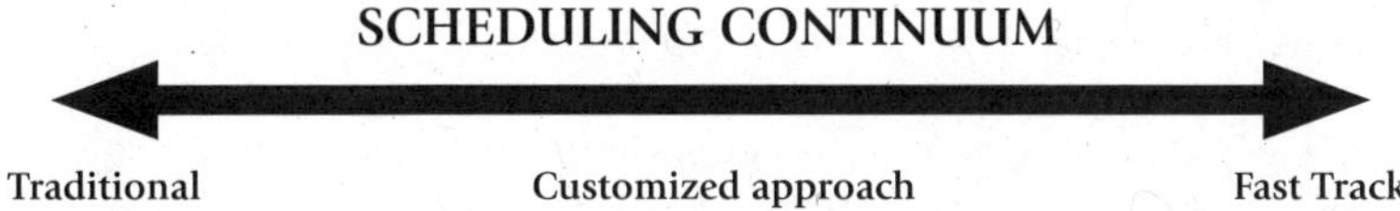

We talk to clients about two scheduling alternatives for organizational improvement with teams: traditional scheduling and fast track scheduling. The typical characteristics of each model are:

Traditional Scheduling

- Meet weekly or every two weeks
- Meet for 1 ½ to 2 hours
- Meet for 3 to 4 months
- Work through the entire process as a team

Fast Track Scheduling

- Prework: Complete issue clarification, process mapping, and data collection in advance
- Two extended (5 to 6 hour) meetings
- First meeting: confirm prework, identify alternatives
- Plan one to two weeks between meetings to evaluate alternatives
- Second meeting: review and select alternative(s), present for sponsor approval, develop implementation plan

These two models are the end points of a continuum of scheduling alternatives. It is up to the team, team leader, and team facilitator to customize their schedule for the best fit with their charge or task, resources, constraints, and concurrent time commitments.

REFERENCES

Bens, I. (1999). *Facilitation at a Glance—A Pocket Guide of Tools & Techniques for Effective Meeting Facilitation*. Association of Quality & Participation/Participation Dynamics.

Brassard, M. and D. Ritter. (1994). *The Memory Jogger II: A Pocket Guide of Tools for Continuous Improvement & Effective Planning*. Methuen, MA: GOAL/QPC.

Scholtes, P. R, Joiner, B., & Streibel, B. (1996). *The Team Handbook: How to Use Teams to Improve Quality* 2nd ed. Madison, WI: Joiner Associates Inc.

Scholtes, P.R. (1998). *The Leader's Handbook*. New York, NY: McGraw-Hill.

Team Memory Jogger, *A Pocket Guide for Team Members* (First Edition) Goal/QPC and Oriel, Inc. (1995).

DOING THE RIGHT THINGS RIGHT: ENHANCED EFFECTIVENESS AND COST SAVINGS

Enhancing academic excellence… enriching the educational experience… aligning missions, programs, and services with fiscal resources… reducing costs. These goals, shared by many higher education institutions, address both effectiveness and efficiency. This chapter explores the concepts of effectiveness and efficiency, the relationship between the two, and how to incorporate both into your planning and improvement initiatives.

EFFECTIVENESS AND EFFICIENCY—BASIC CONCEPTS

Effectiveness is often referred to as *doing the right thing*, while efficiency is *doing things right*.

Effectiveness is an external measure of process output or quality. It can and should be evaluated the way stakeholders, clients, customers, or other recipients of the service or product evaluate it. In the academic environment, effectiveness can be indicated by items such as students learning what they need to know, or providing the optimum mix of cocurricular opportunities. Ineffectiveness can be due to lack of focus, poor communication, or otherwise being out of touch with stakeholders' needs and expectations. Effectiveness is critical for organizational success in a competitive environment. Additionally, in a competitive environment, there may be times when it is necessary to reduce efficiency to achieve effectiveness and meet expectations.

Efficiency is generally thought of as an internal measure of process operations, although improving efficiency may benefit stakeholders as well as the organization. In the academic environment, efficiency areas might include classroom usage, ease and time to register, or textbook availability. Inefficiency can be caused by process errors, inaccessible information, bottlenecks in the process, variation in the process, or costly or non-value added steps in the process. Improving efficiency leads to improved utilization of resources, and can also result in reduced costs or time to deliver a product or service.

Involved in the concepts of effectiveness and efficiency are:

- processes: a sequence of steps or operations that result in an outcome of a product or service; for example planning and teaching a class, or preparing and serving a meal
- organizations: a combination of people, materials, facilities, other resources, and processes that produce products or services; for example, an office, a department, or a library
- stakeholders: those who receive the product or service, or are otherwise interested in the operations and activities of the organization; for example, students, faculty, staff, parents, local residents, or donors

THE RELATIONSHIP BETWEEN EFFECTIVENESS AND EFFICIENCY

Effectiveness comes first in analyzing an organization or process. It is critical to ensure that the services or products being provided are what the stakeholders want and expect. Is an institution providing academic and cocurricluar opportunities consistent with its mission and structure? Only then is it time to look for ways to streamline the processes. If what is being provided is not what stakeholders are expecting or looking for, it doesn't matter how quickly it is delivered or how low the cost. Stakeholders will vote with their feet and go elsewhere.

Effectiveness and Efficiency at Penn State

Penn State is committed to improving those processes, practices, and functions that matter most to its stakeholders through value-added services. As a result of its accreditation process, for example, the university drafted an Assessment Plan for Student Learning and developed an Assessment Academy for faculty. In another example, as a result of internal surveys, Penn State designed development programs for leaders and managers at different levels in their careers. These plans and programs can lead to individual and organizational improvements in both effectiveness and efficiency.

As part of the strategic planning process, Penn State established a Cost Savings Task Force to identify cost savings and opportunities to enhance non-tuition revenue. The goal was to look for ideas that would enable Penn State to continue to provide the same or better level of quality and service (effectiveness) in an environment of limited resources (efficiency).

Using technology, Penn State converted the annual employee benefits process from paper forms to online. This reengineering transformed a manual process to an automated one. Significant cost savings occurred as documents were moved online and printing and postal costs were reduced. Employees across the university now receive more personalized services as individual online entry of benefits data protects privacy and enables benefits office staff to spend their time in benefits counseling instead of data entry.

However, complaints from stakeholders should be viewed as learning and improvement opportunities. Complaints received and process errors indicate opportunities to enhance effectiveness and/or efficiency.

SEIZING OPPORTUNITIES TO IMPROVE EFFECTIVENESS AND EFFICIENCY

How do you capitalize on opportunities to improve effectiveness and efficiency and better serve your stakeholders? The remainder of this chapter provides an overview of a tool and two sets of questions that can help start a conversation about effectiveness and efficiency.

Begin by considering whether what you are doing adds value to your stakeholders and is central to the mission of your unit.

ENHANCING THE EFFECTIVENESS OF YOUR PROGRAMS AND SERVICES

To assess the effectiveness of your programs and services, it may be necessary to learn more about your stakeholders' needs and expectations to determine the extent to which your programs and services directly meet their needs. A thoughtful discussion of the following questions can help you identify programs and services that might benefit from streamlining or redesign. In this discussion, you may also identify activities that could be eliminated because stakeholders no longer find these activities of value or they do not directly contribute to the mission of your unit, and you may identify new programs and services that are needed.

- Who are our key stakeholders or who benefits from services, programs, or products we provide?
- What do our stakeholders require and expect from us?
- What programs and services do we routinely offer or perform?
- What do our stakeholders think about these programs and services? How do we know what they think? Do we have data to support what we think?
- Which of these programs and/or services contribute to the core mission of our unit? Which do not directly contribute?
- How do our programs and/or services directly benefit our stakeholders? How do we know?

STREAMLINING WORK PRACTICES TO GAIN EFFICIENCIES

Often cost savings can be found by identifying routine work practices that have been in place for some time and have not been studied for improvement. Identify where the most resources are being spent and where significant improvement opportunities exist.

Activity-based analysis is one useful tool. Begin by listing all of the major work activities in a week or month, and estimate the amount of time spent on each work activity.

Once you have listed all these activities, select for improvement work activities that:

- Take large amounts of time; or
- Are not productive; or
- Do not add value to the product or service

Once you have determined that an activity is indeed essential to the mission, and streamlining the activity will free up significant resources, the next step is to look for opportunities to make the process more efficient. To begin the conversation about identifying efficiencies, consider these questions:

- Why are things done the way they are? Have we based our decisions on assumptions that are no longer valid? What can we stop doing or do differently?
- What would we change if we were starting from scratch?
- What can we redesign to make faster? Are there bottlenecks, unnecessary wait states, and unnecessary complexity in any of these activities?
- Could any of the activities be done with fewer people?
- How could streamlining or technology make them more efficient?
- What are the resource implications for each of these activities? What does each cost in terms of time, people, equipment, and facilities?
- To what extent do these activities generate revenue or other resources? Are there ways to generate additional revenue to offset the costs?
- Who else offers similar programs and/or services? What opportunities are there for mergers, partnering, or consolidation?

If you identify a large number of improvement opportunities, prioritize them by determining the ease of implementation and the potential payoff from implementation. Look for the easy improvements that will yield "low hanging fruit" as well as a large payoff.

When you have narrowed the number of ideas to a manageable few, create an implementation plan by identifying the specific actions, person responsible, and timeframe for tracking progress. It is also useful to identify measures of success. For example, are you looking to increase stakeholder satisfaction? Reduce complexity? Improve the time for delivery of the service or activity? Improve the quality of the product? If the process or service to be streamlined or redesigned involves more than one person or unit, it is a good idea to form a short-term team of people who know the most about the process or service and who will be responsible for implementing any changes.

DETERMINING THE IMPACT OF YOUR EFFORTS

It is important to measure the impact of your unit's efforts to enhance effectiveness and efficiency. This allows you to gauge the return on your improvement efforts, and also enables you to articulate the success of your efforts to your stakeholders.

To measure the impact of effectiveness and efficiency initiatives, you need pre- and post-measures that are appropriate to your efforts. Efficiency is usually measured more quantitatively. *Financial measures* could include annual or one-time cost savings, increased revenue, or reduced space needs. *Time saved,* measured through the reduction of cycle time and the elimination of steps in your unit's processes, can also be measured financially in terms of pay and benefits for the time saved, but should be thought of as freeing resources to work on other initiatives and improvements. *Stakeholder satisfaction,* often determined through the use of surveys, interviews, and focus groups, could include measures of student learning or alumni surveys, and indicates the effectiveness of your product or service delivery. Don't forget to measure the satisfaction of your unit's faculty and staff (internal stakeholders) as well as stakeholders external to your unit.

FAST TRACK TO PROCESS SIMPLIFICATION

Are you looking for a faster way to make long-lasting improvements in your unit? Do you want to simplify a process to reduce time and costs? Are you planning to use technology to automate a process? Do you want to give your customers access to self-service on the Web? The Fast Track approach can help you meet these goals.

WHAT IS FAST TRACK IMPROVEMENT?

The Fast Track approach was developed to address the opportunity to continually improve the improvement process itself and to help ensure successful implementation of high impact projects. The model is adapted from the Fast Cycle Change model developed by Dr. Ian Hau (1997), which substantially reduces the amount of time required to complete a process improvement/redesign project by anticipating implementation needs, completing tasks in parallel, eliminating time delays, and reducing the amount of review and repetition that occurs when teams meet infrequently over several months.

Hau has demonstrated that short project duration and high impact actually go together (1997). He describes four principles that help ensure project success:

1. Articulate the desired impact when planning the project.
2. Focus on the transition when assembling the team and designing process changes.
3. Keep process changes simple, with three to six features.

4. Focus on the process of assembling "knowledge parts" rather than the parts themselves.

Hau recommends mocking up the completion report when formulating the project as an effective way to help visualize what the team aims to accomplish and to identify the gap between the current and ideal processes. He also notes that to maximize ownership for implementation, it is crucial to choose team members from among those that will be implementing the change.

Using the Fast Track approach, a team can quickly streamline a process and implement improvements that will last. Teams identify and reduce inefficiencies such as bottlenecks, rework, and other time delays. They reduce complexities that result when several people handle the same task, or when there are unnecessary layers of approval. They look for opportunities to perform activities in parallel and other sequence changes that will simplify processes. They attempt to eliminate overlapping paper and electronic processing.

Much of the Fast Track project is completed outside team meetings, saving valuable team time for the work of the actual redesign. The total project, from project approval to demonstration of impact, will be completed within 17 to 22 weeks with only a fraction of that time used for team meetings. Following the project's end, the process owner will continue to monitor performance measures.

FROM INITIATION TO DEMONSTRATION OF IMPACT

Step one, *Initiation*, should be completed within four to five weeks, with the majority of work in this phase done by the team leader and facilitator. It is crucial to choose a project that is important to stakeholders and is expected to achieve high impact. It is also important to choose team members who will also be implementing the project to ensure widespread participation and ownership. The initiation step has a significant impact on the successful implementation of solutions.

Steps two and three, *Design Phase One and Two*, are typically completed within three weeks after the completion of step one. A team will often schedule a day-long meeting for each of the design phases, with a week between meetings to analyze potential solutions. All team members do work in these steps.

Step four, *Implementation and Demonstration of Impact*, should be completed within 11 to 15 weeks. The work in this step should be

Figure 12.1—The Fast Track Model

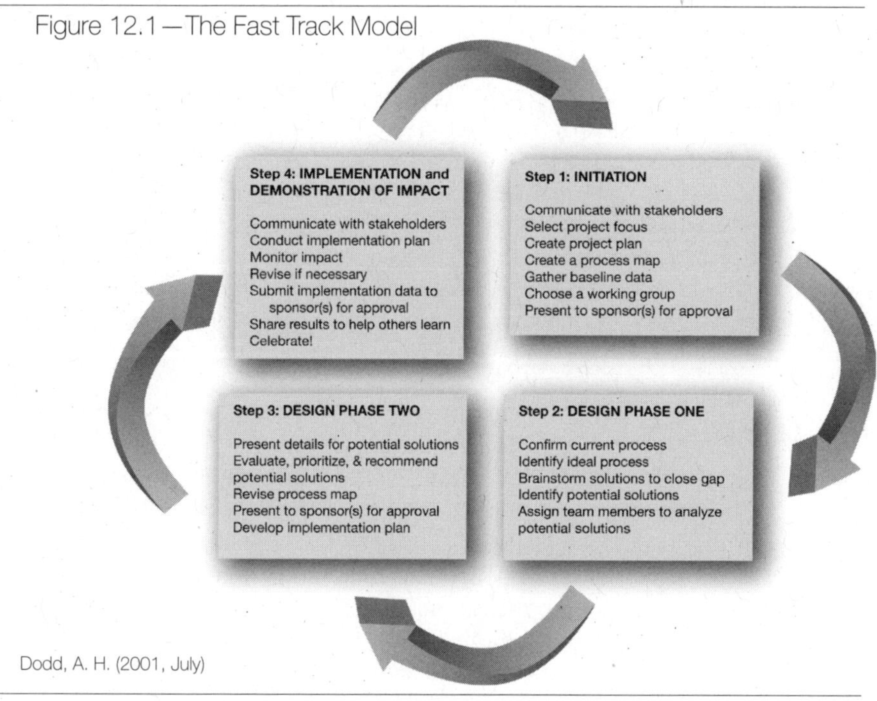

Dodd, A. H. (2001, July)

coordinated by the team leader and conducted by all team members. The team leader should communicate regularly with those conducting the implementation, and should schedule short project review meetings if appropriate. At the end of this step, data on the impact of the redesigned processes should be submitted to team sponsor(s).

REFERENCES

Baldrige National Quality Program. (current year). Education Criteria for Performance Excellence. www.quality.nist.gov.

Brassard, M. and D. Ritter. (1994). *The Memory Jogger II: A Pocket Guide of Tools for Continuous Improvement & Effective Planning*. Methuen, MA: GOAL/QPC.

Dodd, A. H. (2001, July). Fast Track to Process Simplification at Penn State. Presented at the National Consortium for Continuous Improvement annual conference, New York City.

Hau, I. and F. Calhoun. (1997). Fast Cycle Change in Knowledge-Based Organizations: Building Fundamental Capability for Implementing Strategic Transformation. *Center for Quality and Productivity Improvement Report No. 161*, University of Wisconsin, Madison, WI.

Scholtes, P.R., B. Joiner, and B. Streibel. (2003). *The Team Handbook: How to Use Teams to Improve Quality* (3rd ed.). Madison, WI: Oriel Inc.

The Fast Track Approach in Action

OUTREACH COMMUNICATIONS used the Fast Track approach to redesign the *Outreach Magazine* production process. They were able to increase their publication schedule to add an additional issue. "The CQI Fast Track approach provided a flexible and time efficient way to streamline our *Outreach Magazine* production process. We assembled our team from several Outreach Units and we had multiple responsibilities to manage and tight deadlines to meet. This approach enabled us to meet our deadlines for production of the magazine and improve our processes simultaneously. It has been two years since we implemented the CQI approach and we continue to examine our processes and apply the guiding principles to our work. The Fast Track approach was perfect for our team!"

—Tracey Huston,
Director of Outreach Communications,
Outreach & Cooperative Extension

PENN STATE ALTOONA used the Fast Track approach to redesign the process used to inform students of faculty course cancellations. "I was especially pleased with the Fast Track process. I am usually interested in solving an identified problem as quickly as possible; this process provides the opportunity to do so. I realize that Fast Track is not appropriate for all issues/problems that one needs to address, but I would use it as much as possible. I believe that the team members who worked on our Fast Track project were also pleased. They felt a true sense of accomplishment, and were particularly pleased that they could identify the problem, draft potential solution(s), and have those solution(s) implemented in a relatively short time frame."

—Richard K. Shaffer,
Director of Admissions and Enrollment Services,
Penn State Altoona

LIBRARIES' MEDIA & TECHNOLOGY SUPPORT SERVICES used the Fast Track approach to reduce errors. "The Fast Track was definitely the best approach for our group. Media & Technology Support Services has 34 full-time employees, including 21 technical service employees. Since we are a service group, it is extremely difficult to schedule group meetings during fall and spring semesters. By using the Fast Track method, we were able to meet a minimum number of times to get to the heart of our issues and concerns."

—William Bishop,
Media & Technology Support Services,
University Libraries

OUTREACH MARKETING used the Fast Track approach to reduce by over 50% the time it takes them to produce print publications. "I would have to say that Fast Track was probably the best approach for our team because we are accustomed to working in a fast-paced environment, and expect visible results within a short time. Had we taken the more traditional, long-term approach, the team would have burned out. Also, we were fortunate that we already had the data to show what was actually happening, so we didn't need to spend time collecting and analyzing it. If there is a negative aspect to Fast Track it is this: The change effort does not build up a lot of momentum, so it is easy to experience a drop in energy and motivation. You really have to have a strong driver to keep things moving once you're in the implementation phase."

—Angela Rogers,
Senior Marketing Associate,
Outreach & Cooperative Extension

LEADING UNIT LEVEL PLANNING

Issues you can address through the integration of planning, improvement, and assessment:

"We need to identify areas of excellence in which we should invest over the next few years."

"Our resources are declining and we need to determine how to maintain our quality standards."

"We want to adapt what we do to implement our new strategies."

"We need to update our undergraduate program."

"We need to be competitive in attracting new faculty."

"We need to solve our enrollment and space issues."

"We have lots of data but we aren't using it to improve our programs."

STARTING A STRATEGIC PLANNING INITIATIVE

Many faculty and staff are aware of strategic planning, but are not clear on how to successfully approach the process. Even seasoned leaders may have questions such as the following:

What exactly is strategic planning?

Bryson (1995) defines strategic planning as "... a disciplined effort to produce fundamental decisions and actions that shape and guide what an organization is, what it does, and why it does it" (p. 4).

Strategic planning will help you and your colleagues identify where you want your institution to be in the future and what you need to do to get there.

What are effective models and approaches?

Effective strategic planning approaches include several common elements. These are not always completed in the same order, and the approach you use should be tailored to your unit's culture and needs.

Common elements often include the assessment of internal strengths and weaknesses, and external opportunities and threats; the identification of values, mission, vision, and goals; the identification of strategies and performance measures; and the development, implementation, and periodic review of action plans.

Figure 13.1 illustrates a model developed by Penn State's Office of Planning and Institutional Assessment for use as a guide when designing a planning process.

Figure 13.1—The Penn State Model for Integrating Planning, Improvement, and Assessment

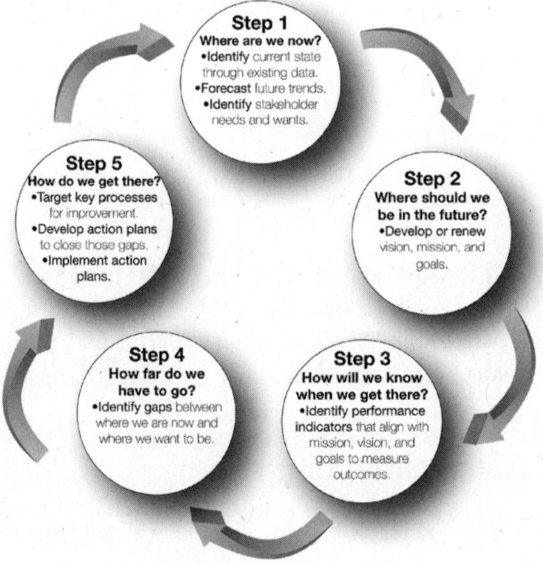

How do we prepare for, build, and implement a strategic plan?

Often, a unit leader will initiate the planning process by meeting with a facilitator/consultant to plan a retreat or series of discussions. The leader will assure that assessment data are available to inform the planning process. Discussion(s) will be held with stakeholders to identify the unit's priorities, and to determine how to achieve these priorities.

Implementation will follow, with regular progress reviews. It is important to develop an implementation schedule with an expected completion date and intermediate steps and dates.

Figures 13.2, 13.3, and 13.4 on the following pages illustrate examples of three planning approaches, based on unit size and scheduling preferences. There is no one right way to do unit planning; design an approach that fits your institution's culture and needs.

Information in the final plan will probably fall into three categories: background and analysis (the unit's current state), goals and measures (where the unit wants to go), and strategies and actions (how the unit will get there).

Who should participate, and how?

Faculty, staff, and others with responsibility for implementing the plan should be engaged in the planning process. A small group, with less than 15 members, may be able to involve all members in the planning process. A larger unit, with several departments, will need to identify an approach to provide all members an opportunity for feedback and involvement. The leader should also identify a means to provide administrators with information on the unit's planning process, and receive feedback during the process to ensure alignment and support.

How should we initiate the process?

Begin where you are, with the data you have. Planning is as much a process of engagement as it is a matter of data analysis. It is also an iterative process. Look at your plan as a dynamic document that is a guide to your routine activities, prioritization, and resource allocation as well as a longer-term guide that can be revised and updated as your situation or environment evolves.

Figure 13.2—Sample Approach for a Unit with Fewer than Ten Members. Incorporates Planning into Weekly 90-Minute Staff Meetings Over Three Months.

Week 1	• Review – Strategic planning concepts – Standard terminology of the field • Draft mission and vision statements • Identify stakeholder populations and their perceived expectations
Week 2	• Review – Unit values, mission, and vision statement – Timeline for developing strategic plan • Develop interview protocol for stakeholder organizations
Week 3	• Review stakeholder interview protocol • Begin stakeholder interviews
Week 4	• Review – Progress with stakeholder interviews – Historical data already compiled • Plan additional customer (student) data gathering
Week 5	• Develop schedule for customer (student) focus groups • Review available data banks for focus group questions
Week 6	• Review interview data and target key interest/ improvement areas • Review focus group protocol • Develop outline of strategic plan
Week 7	• Begin work on goals and measures
Week 8	• Conduct focus groups
Week 9	• Review data from focus groups • Target key interest/improvement areas
Week 10	• Finalize goals and measures • Begin work on strategies and actions • Draft background/analysis of strategic plan
Week 11	• Continue work on strategies and actions • Draft goals and measures of strategic plan
Week 12	• Draft strategies and actions section of strategic plan
Week 13	• Draft of complete strategic plan available for review

Figure 13.3— Sample Approach for a Unit with Fewer than 10 Members Using a Day-Long Planning Retreat Plus Pre-Work and Follow-Up

Retreat Preparation Two Hours	• Establish ground rules for retreat • Review unit mission and discuss vision • Review current barriers • Review strategic planning process • Confirm direction for full day retreat • Identify action items (information to be distributed before retreat)
Retreat All Day	• Identify unit strengths and challenges, both internal and external (individuals complete strengths, weaknesses, opportunities, and challenges matrix individually prior to retreat) • Develop desired image of unit 2 to 3 years in the future • Based on strengths, challenges, and desired image, identify key issues/ goals for unit • Identify current position of unit for each of these key issues • Identify which issues are drivers • Develop initial list of possible strategies for each key issue
Follow-up Half Day	• Develop additional strategies for key issues • Review issues and strategies based on - long- or short-term approaches - priority - whether within unit's control
Remaining Actions	• Meet with unit leader's administrator to review unit direction • Develop draft plan • Identify detailed actions to implement strategies

Figure 13.4—Sample Approach for Larger Unit with Several Departments. Incorporates Information Sharing

	Activity
Manager and Department Heads (3 hours)	• Review strategic planning concepts • Discuss values, mission, vision • Identify unit stakeholders • List possible strategies and actions • Plan next steps
Entire staff (30 minutes)	• Present strategic planning approach • Present department goals • Answer questions
Manager/Dept Heads (1 hour)	• Department Heads provide written department goals to each other and Manager
Between meetings	• Manager provides feedback to Department Heads on department goals • Department Heads get input from their staff on mission and vision
Manager/Dept Heads (1 hour)	• Manager provides draft of strategic plan • Department Heads bring departmental input • Department Heads bring prioritized list of departmental goals and strategies
Between meetings	• Manager revises and distributes draft • Department Heads share plan with staff and get feedback
Manager/Dept Heads (30 minutes)	• Review draft of strategic plan
Between meetings	• Department Heads and staff develop actions to implement strategies
Entire staff (30 minutes)	• Present strategic plan • Answer questions
Remaining actions	• Present plan to administrator with unit oversight

A PLANNING CHECKLIST

The following checklist has been developed from the Strategic Planning component of the Baldrige National Quality Program Education Criteria for Performance Excellence (National Institute of Standards and Technology, 2007):

- Establish a process for planning
- Gather and analyze data related to:
  - Student, stakeholder, and market needs and expectations
  - Local, regional, or national economics and demographics
  - Organizational capabilities and resources, including time, funds, facilities, and people
  - Education and technology trends
  - Disciplinary trends
  - Benchmarks and comparative data from peer organizations
- Identify key goals and objectives that align with institutional goals, and a timeframe for accomplishing them
- Identify key performance measures and targets for the goals and objectives
- Develop and implement specific action plans to accomplish goals and objectives, and identify a way to monitor the action plans and modify them as needed

You may also find the "Are We Making Progress?," "Are We Making Progress as Leaders?," and "easy Insight: Take a First Step Toward a Baldrige Self-Assessment" surveys, all available at the Baldrige National Quality Program Web site (http://www.quality.nist.gov/), useful in your planning process.

REFERENCES

Bryson, John M. (1995). *Strategic Planning for Public and Nonprofit Organizations—A Guide to Strengthening and Sustaining Organizational Achievement* (Revised Edition). San Francisco, CA: Jossey-Bass.

Dolence, Michael G., Daniel J. Rowley, Herman D. Lugan. (1997). *Working Toward Strategic Change: A Step-by-Step Guide to the Planning Process*. San Francisco, CA: Jossey-Bass.

Melum, Mara Minerva, and Casey Collett. (2000). *Breakthrough Leadership: Achieving Organizational Alignment Through Hoshin Planning*. Salem, NH: GOAL/QPC.

National Institute of Standards and Technology Baldrige National Quality Program. (2007). Education Criteria for Performance Excellence. www.baldrige.nist.gov.

Society for College and University Planning Web site, www.scup.org.

Schwartz, Peter. (1991) *The Art of the Long View: Planning for the Future in an Uncertain World*. New York, NY: Currency Doubleday.

DMADV: AN APPROACH FOR DEVELOPING NEW INITIATIVES

This chapter provides an overview of the DMADV (Define, Measure, Analyze, Design, Verify) approach for design and implementation of new services, products, or processes. Because of its thorough analysis, basis in data, and early identification of measures of success, DMADV can be a useful approach in implementing new initiatives or strategies to accomplish planning goals.

As technology has advanced over the past 20 years, and made greater data collection and analysis possible, there has been increasing emphasis on basing decisions on data, and on more detailed data. DMADV is one aspect of Design for Six Sigma (DFSS), which has evolved from the earlier approaches of Continuous Quality Improvement (CQI) and Motorola's "Six Sigma"[1] approach to reduce variation. DFSS emphasizes more structure and metrics than earlier CQI, with a greater focus on the bottom line, but uses many of the improvement tools. The intent of *Design for Six Sigma (DFSS)* is to

- minimize future problems
- minimize variability
- maximize satisfaction
- deliver what is desired in a timely fashion
- include suppliers in the design process

[1]Six Sigma is a registered trademark and service mark of Motorola, Inc. It is based on standard deviation, a measure of variation, and refers to control of variation that results in only 3.4 defects or errors out of a million items produced.

Within DFSS, there are two approaches to plan change and reduce variation: DMAIC (Define, Measure, Analyze, Improve, Control) to improve *existing* situations or processes; and DMADV (Define, Measure, Analyze, Design, Verify) to design a *new* service, product, or process. Both DMAIC and DMADV are similar to Penn State's IMPROVE model for improvement, but focus more on data and analysis. The DMADV approach was designed to develop a service, product, or process that will successfully address identified issues and maintain it through normal operations. A top-level decision is needed to drive and support the DMADV project, and this can be one basis for its link to strategy implementation. From another perspective, implementing strategies identified in a long-range or strategic plan often involves introducing new services, products, or processes and procedures. Because of its focus on success through thorough analysis, DMADV may be a useful approach to strategy implementation.

There are five major steps to the **DMADV** approach, and component steps to each of those five. A key component of the DMADV approach is an active "toll gate" check sheet review of the outcomes of each of the five steps before proceeding to the next one.

Step 1: Define. Identify purpose, identify and set measurable goals from the perspective of both the organization and stakeholder, develop schedule and guidelines for review, identify and assess risks.

Step 2: Measure. Define requirements, define market segments, identify critical parameters for design, design scorecards to evaluate design components that are critical to quality (CTQ), reassess risks, assess production process capability and product capability.

Step 3: Analyze. Develop design alternatives, identify the best combination of requirements to provide value within constraints, develop conceptual designs, evaluate, select the best components and develop the best available design.

Step 4: Design. Develop a high-level design, develop exact specifications, develop detailed component designs, develop related processes, optimize design.

Step 5: Verify. Validate that the design is acceptable to all stakeholders, complete pilot test, confirm expectations, expand deployment, document lessons learned.

These steps employ many of the same tools used in improvement initiatives and project management. The references listed on page 104 can provide information on more complex tools.

Using DMADV in an Academic Setting

The president at the University of Miami wanted a more residential campus. Growth in enrollment and a requirement for first-year students to live on campus resulted in a housing shortage. Analysis indicated that new housing would have greater impact on the president's objectives than renovating existing housing, so the strategic decision was made to design and build new housing for the business school.

In the Define phase, the team reviewed the background that led to the decision to build housing and completed an analysis of the risks involved with the project, identifying two major risks: 1) the building would become obsolete and 2) there would be difficulty in the interaction of design team members. They also analyzed the benefits of the project. Then they developed a plan for the project that addressed the opportunity (to advance in school rankings), the objectives (high class living facilities for executive, graduate, and upper-class undergraduate business students), the scope (timelines and location), and the measures of success (increase in on-campus residents).

For the Measurement phase, the team divided their prospective residents into different segments (executive, graduate, and upper-class undergraduate business students) and gathered data on their expectations for a new living facility. For example, would they be surprised and delighted by, expect and like, or not like items such as a queen-sized bed, a large corner desk, a microwave, or laundry service? How much (in terms of percentage increase in total cost) would they be willing to pay for each of these amenities?

In the Analyze phase, five different designs were generated, based on inputs from undergraduate and graduate populations and combinations of their preferences. Designs were then analyzed based on data indicating willingness to pay more, repair frequency, ease of repair, ease to clean, replacement frequency, and cost/benefit ratio. A risk analysis was conducted for the risks of personal injury or fire. As a result of the analysis, a final design was selected and during Design detailed floor plans were developed for the residence facility. Finally, as part of the Verification process, the plans were provided to university stakeholders to get buy in for developing a transition plan to proceed with the project. (Johnson 2006)

DEFINE

The Define function establishes a clear definition of the project. This includes the product or process that will be improved or the needs that will be met, and the scope of the project, with a schedule, resources, and deliverables, much like a project management plan. It includes a change plan, to identify and document who or what components of the organization will be impacted by the change, to what extent, and how receptive or resistant they may be to the change. It also includes a risk management plan, identifying the known and foreseeable risks in the project, for example: technical (complex design); human (stakeholder resistance); team (low commitment by team members); planning (inadequate design research); business (cost increase); organizational and political (too many decision makers, inadequate sponsorship). Once risks are identified, an analysis is done of the degree of seriousness of each risk and the means to address or minimize each risk.

MEASURE

Measure focuses on customer (or student, client, or stakeholder) requirements. Who are the different groups of clients or stakeholders who may have different interests? What exactly are these people looking for in the new product or service? What is the relative importance or value of the different components they would like to see in the new product or service? Data is used to identify the "must haves" in the product or service, those things that are critical to quality (CTQ) from the client's point of view. There is also an attempt to determine and prioritize the individual return on investment (ROI) for each component. As more data is gathered, risks can be reassessed.

ANALYZE

The analysis focuses on identification of the different approaches that could be used to meet customer or stakeholder requirements. Key functions within the requirements are prioritized. Alternative methods and processes are developed based on prioritization of these functions. Finally, several alternatives are evaluated, and the most effective alternative, based on the best parts of the best concepts, is selected for design. During the Analyze stage, an estimate of the total life cycle cost of the design is made, including costs for development of the concept, creation of the production system or process, ongoing production, use of the product or service, disposal of the product or service, and final retirement of the process or production system.

DESIGN

The Design stage includes both a high-level and detailed design for the selected alternative. Design elements are prioritized and a high-level design is developed. Following that, a more detailed model is prototyped. There is also an effort to identify where errors may occur and address them through modifications.

VERIFY

The final step involves piloting the new product or service, gathering data and evaluating performance, satisfaction, or results. Based on the data, any final adjustments are made. A plan is developed and implemented to transition the product or service to a routine operation for the organization and ensure that the change is maintained. Finally, lessons learned in the DMADV process are documented.

IMPLEMENTING DMADV

At different levels of an organization or aspects of an initiative, there may be more emphasis on some components of the DMADV approach than others. There may be different teams assembled to address different parts of the initiative. Define, Measure, and Verify may be the focus at the system or administrative level. At the unit, subsystem, or module level, emphasis may be on Measure, Analyze, and Design. In these cases, communication between the different groups, and documentation, supported by the DMADV toll gate check lists, is critical.

The goal of the DMADV approach is to produce what is needed to successfully address the identified issue with the initially identified desired results, and maintain it through normal operations.

REFERENCES

Ginn, D., Streibel, B., and Varner, E. (2004). *The Design for Six Sigma Memory Jogger.* Salem, NH: Goal/QPC.

Gitlow, H. S., Levine, D. M., and Popovich, E. A. (2006). *Design for Six Sigma for Green Belts and Champions: Applications for Service Operations—Foundations, Tools, DMADV, Cases, and Certification.* Upper Saddle River, NJ: Pearson: Prentice Hall.

Johnson, J. A., Gitlow, H., Widener, S., and Popovich, E. (2006). "Designing New Housing at the University of Miami: A 'Six Sigma' DMADV/DFSS Case Study," *Quality Engineering,* 18: 299-323. Oxford, England: Taylor and Francis Group, LLC.

TOOLS FOR PLANNING, ASSESSMENT, AND IMPROVEMENT

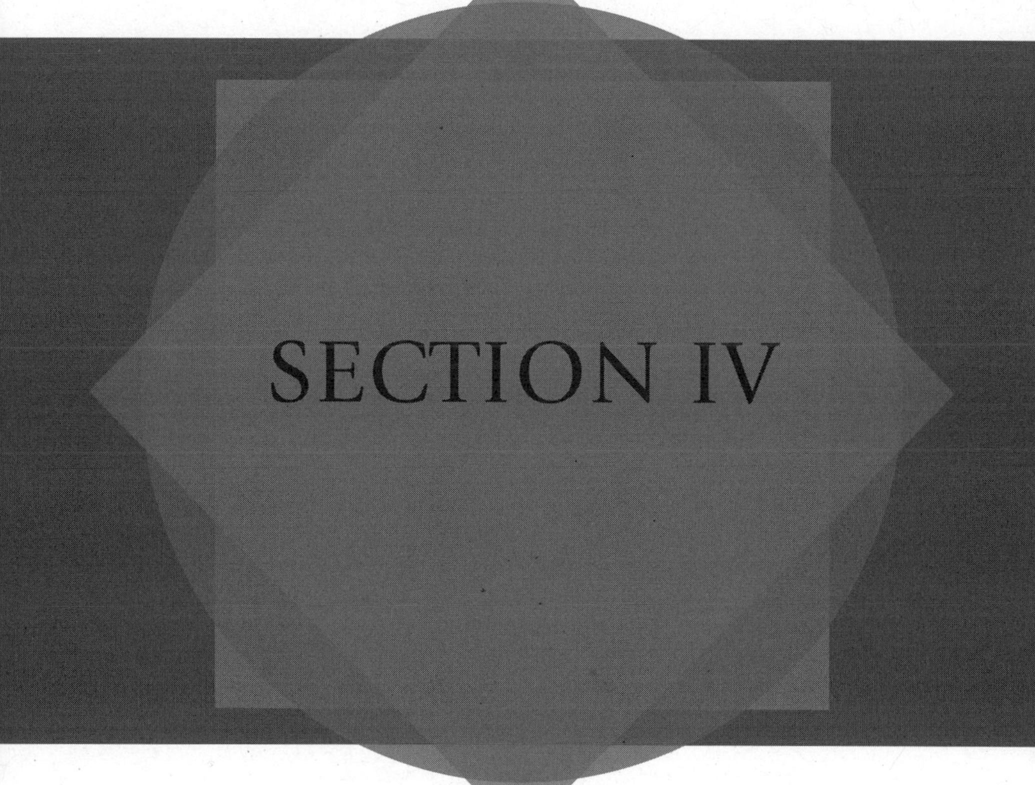

DEVELOPING STRATEGIC PERFORMANCE INDICATORS

The focus in strategic planning is often on getting the plan written. However, the purpose of planning is not to develop goals but to accomplish them. One way to know whether you have accomplished a goal is to measure performance. This chapter provides some tips on how to select measures and indicators that can help you to:

- identify your starting point
- monitor and measure progress
- know whether you are headed in the right direction
- know when you have achieved the goal or closed the gap between where you are now and where you want to be in the future

COMPONENTS OF PLANNING

Measures and indicators are a key component of any basic planning model. As shown below, at the core of the planning process are the organization's values, its mission (why it exists), and its vision (where it wants to be in the future or how it wants to be viewed). Goals are the path to that future vision. Specific strategies, actions, and improvement initiatives will need to be incorporated into the operational activities of the organization to reach the goals. Measures of performance and strategic indicators will show the progress the organization is making.

Figure15.1—Components of Planning

CRITERIA FOR DEVELOPING MEASURES AND INDICATORS

The key to selecting measures and indicators is asking thoughtful questions about how important accomplishments can be measured in an understandable manner with data that can be collected using a reasonable amount of resources.

The following criteria, developed by Penn State, can be customized to fit an institution-wide or departmental focus. The specificity of the measure will be influenced by the level within the organization at which the plan is being developed.

1. Does the measure reflect an important performance dimension?
2. Are data on this measure likely to lead to improvement?
3. Does the measure reflect stakeholders' needs?
4. Do key stakeholders view the measure as credible?

5. Can the measure be communicated to and understood by a wide audience?
6. Is the direction clear? That is, would an increase be clearly desirable or undesirable?
7. Is the cost/benefit relationship sensible (in terms of data availability or resources needed to collect data versus value)?
8. Can those accountable for providing the data be identified?
9. Will the measure be sustainable over a period of years?

MEASURES AND INDICATORS WITHIN AN ORGANIZATION

Developing good measures in planning can take some planning of its own. The initial data-based assessment and analysis that led to the establishment of goals and strategies should provide a starting point or guidance in the determination of meaningful measures and indicators. While goals should be aligned, or consistent, throughout an organization, actual goals, indicators, measures, strategies, and actions will be influenced by a department or unit's location in the organization. The table below shows how a common goal could be implemented differently throughout an institution.

Figure 15.2—Implementing a Goal Through the Institution

	University	College	Department
Goal	Enhance Academic Excellence	Enhance Academic Excellence	Enhance Academic Excellence
Strategic Performance Indicator	Quality of Incoming Students	Quality of Faculty	Quality of Discipline or Program
Measures of Performance	Mean SAT and GRE Scores	Number of Publications in Selected Journals	Improved Mean Scores on Certification Exams
Strategies, Processes, Actions, Targets	Target Schools for Recruiting	Promote Cluster Hiring	Identify Learning Objectives and a Plan for Assessment

SMART GOALS

How you state your goals and strategies can help you determine what to measure. A commonly known acronym for developing goals and plans, SMART, identifies five characteristics of an effective goal:

S specific

M measurable

A achievable

R relevant

T time and resource based

First, the goal should be something that can be reached, be *achievable*. It should also be *relevant*, worth the resources the accomplishment of the goal will consume. The terms realistic, results-oriented, or resource-based can also be paired with the R in the acronym.

The three remaining components of SMART all relate to measurement. The specificity and time-based aspects incorporate data related to accomplishment. For example, to have better prepared new students a *specific* goal could be to "Improve student orientation" through specific strategies such as "Increasing information about student orientation events" or "Ensuring all have access to timely information about student orientation events" rather than simply "Improving communication about student orientation events." *Time* is addressed by stating that improvements will be in place by a particular date, such as a week before students arrive on campus for the fall semester.

Once the specific goal and/or strategies have been identified, with an implementation date, the actual *measure needs to be identified.* There are many options: a simple "Yes" or "No" to indicate whether the information was accessible; a measure, such as a Web counter to indicate the number of visits to the information site; or a survey to indicate what number or percent of a population was aware of the information. Other factors contributing to the goal of improved student orientation could be the result of activities to redesign, restructure, or change the timing of the events.

Performance measures and indicators are tools for organizational learning, communication, strategic change, and improvement. It can take time to identify possible measures and then evaluate them. This time and effort should be viewed as an investment that will yield a significant return in the future. First, development of measures and indicators at the start of the planning process will increase the likelihood of having baseline data, which identifies a starting point and makes measurement of progress toward a goal easier. Second, having data-based goals will provide information on how much progress toward a goal has been made, and will make it possible to clearly define when a goal has been accomplished.

REFERENCES

The Pennsylvania State University. "Strategic Indicators: Measuring and Improving University Performance." Current edition at http://www.psu.edu/president/pia/indicators/index.htm.

EFFECTIVE MEETINGS

Meetings often get off track, or consist of rambling discussions with no decisions or outcomes. This chapter focuses on the elements of effective meetings and the models and tools a meeting leader can use to increase the likelihood of a productive meeting.

MEETING BASICS

Time is valuable and cannot be replaced once it is gone. For that reason, whenever people come together for a meeting, it is important that the meeting purpose be accomplished as efficiently and effectively as possible.

Meetings can be thought of as falling into one or more of several categories:

- Informational—getting information out and answering questions
- Exploratory—gathering ideas about possibilities
- Decision making—evaluating and selecting alternatives
- Progress reports—tracking work on ongoing projects

Groups may meet once, or may meet on an ongoing basis, such as a regular staff meeting or a project management group, in which case they incur some maintenance or housekeeping activities. In either case the group has a specific purpose for meeting, or the person calling the meeting has a specific reason for getting this group of people together.

The elements of an effective meeting include:

- An agenda
- Planned time for each item on the agenda
- Advance identification of the person responsible for presenting each item on the agenda
- A record of the meeting—a timely summary of key discussion points, decisions, action items (who will follow up on what and when, though not necessarily who said what), and remaining open issues

If the group will be meeting on an ongoing basis, group members will need to decide how they are sharing ongoing responsibilities and what they can expect from each other. This can include how the minute or note taker will be determined (for example, rotating in first name alphabetical order), and what the format of the minutes will be (to simplify writing the minutes). Several of the references listed, and many office software packages, provide templates for planning meetings and recording the minutes. An ongoing group will also need to decide what constitutes a quorum at a meeting, so that those not present accept the decisions made by those who were there and are ready to move on at the next meeting. Ground rules can address issues such as starting and ending meetings on time and not interrupting each other. For a group with ongoing meetings, at the end of one meeting the group members should be able to determine the agenda for the next meeting.

In *How to Make Meetings Work*, a classic guide to planning and managing successful and productive meetings, Doyle and Straus identify five ingredients of an effective meeting (p.32):

1. Common focus on content
2. Common focus on process
3. Someone responsible for maintaining an open and balanced communication flow
4. Someone responsible for protecting individuals from personal attack
5. Clearly defined and agreed upon roles and responsibilities for all involved

The common thread in this list is an individual in charge of the meeting who maintains focus and manages communication and activities within the meeting. This may be the group leader, committee chair, or an external facilitator.

MEETING MODELS

It is important that all participants know what type of meeting they are attending—sharing information, gathering ideas, making a decision, tracking progress, or some combination of these. In a decision-making meeting it is also important that both the leader and meeting attendees are clear who will be making the decision, and how.

Tannenbaum and Schmidt's model of a decision-making continuum in "How to Choose a Leadership Pattern" is useful. At one end of the continuum, the leader may make the decision with no input from the group. At the other end of the continuum, the group may make the decision with little or no input from the leader. Between these two points are situations where the leader will make a decision based on discussion with the group, the leader and group will jointly make a decision, or the group will make a decision within parameters defined by the leader.

If both the leader and group are not clear at the start of the meeting about what type of meeting they are having, or where they are on the decision-making continuum, the result may be an ineffective meeting or angry and frustrated meeting participants. Where on this continuum the decision making lies may have an impact on how the leader chooses to lead the meeting. If the group will be making the decision, they need to determine in advance the approach they will use to make the decision, whether it is reaching consensus through open discussion, multivoting to prioritize alternatives, or another option.

A first step for effective meeting and planning is using the SMART approach. Meeting goals or outcomes (whether they be sharing information, identifying alternatives, reaching a decision, or developing an action plan) should be:

S specific
M measurable
A achievable
R relevant
T time and resource based

Figure 16.1—Planning for Energetic Meetings

What...? is the goal is it - specific - measurable - attainable - what we want to accomplish - worthy of the effort do we need to know or explore feelings do we have about the goal	**Who...?** is excited about the goal will be responsible else is involved is the audience must be informed can help may hinder
How...? will we achieve the goal can we generate or maintain enthusiasm will we demonstrate we have achieved the goal	**When...?** must we achieve the goal are the intermediary steps or deadlines do we return to the group with a problem

Source: Marshall's Energetic Meetings

There are several models the leader can use to help implement this approach and manage the meeting, either informally or formally.

Plan and Run Your Meeting Like A Reporter

One approach the leader can use to plan and manage meetings effectively follows the guide for writing a newspaper article—keep asking what, who, how, and when. Marshall's Energetic Meetings (see Figure 16.1) expands on this. The leader can use these checklists as he or she manages a group discussion to make sure all necessary items are covered.

A Developmental Approach to Meetings

In *Team-Managed Facilitation*, Kinlaw defines a successful meeting as one in which:

- All tasks are performed effectively and efficiently

- The group has further developed and ensured capacity to continue to produce excellent results
- The group meeting is consciously viewed as an object of continuous improvement

The continually improving meeting implies that the group will be meeting on an ongoing basis; Kinlaw's guides for leader intervention can be used at individual meetings. The model has three stages: *potential, performance,* and *results.* Results depend on the potential brought to the meeting and performance during the meeting. The model also identifies functions the leader can fill at each stage to help the group have a successful meeting and improve their meeting skills.

Potential is what the group starts with. This is composed of both resources and structures. Resources are what the group has—the right people, commitment, preparation, access to information, facilities and equipment, time, external support, communication, and problem-solving skills. The leader helps the group clarify what resources it has and needs. Structures are related to the long-term strategy of the group and how it operates—roles, norms, decision-making methods, goals, tools, and processes. The leader helps the group identify and address related questions—ground rules, for one.

The group's *performance* is the result of how they use those resources to meet, communicate, and achieve understanding. Rational processes include short-term tactics such as the flow of meetings and using a structured approach. The leader can help the group identify an approach or process, such as a meeting agenda or the Plan-Do-Check-Act or IMPROVE model, and follow its steps. Effective communication supports development and use of resources, structure, and rational process. Effective communication is:

- Appropriate—timely and relevant
- Concrete—including data, and specific examples
- Respectful—using active listening
- Team centered—focusing on group goals

Effective communication is not generalizing, ridiculing, judging, or blaming team members or others. Through effective communication, the leader keeps the group aware of what it's doing and ensures the group makes conscious decisions. Understanding on the part of group members results from using rational processes and effective communication to gather, examine, and evaluate data and alternatives.

Group *results* include the accomplishment of the task, development of the group, and more effective meetings. In Kinlaw's model, the leader decides when to intervene in group discussions or activities based on three criteria:

- Listening to understand: Is the leader hearing what was said, not what was expected or assumed?
- Modeling quality communications: Is the communication group centered, focusing on group, not individual, needs?
- Keeping the group conscious: Is the group on track? Are members aware of the decisions they are making or not making?

As the group becomes more mature, its members take on the behaviors the facilitator has modeled and the leader has a lesser role.

EVALUATING MEETINGS

As Kinlaw's model shows, while the group and leader are working on a specific meeting topic or project, they have opportunities to make their meetings more effective. To do this, they need data about how effective the meetings are. The first question to be answered in evaluating meetings is: What exactly are you going to evaluate?

- Who are you going to evaluate?
    - Yourself (each group member evaluate themselves)
    - Your group leader/facilitator
    - Your whole group
- What are you going to evaluate?
    - Meeting content
    - Group process
- How are you going to do the evaluation?
    - As a whole group, or individually
    - Via discussion or survey (paper or online)

In one quick approach, the group discusses what went well and what they could do differently next time, developing two lists. This is often called the "plus/delta" approach, with a "+" heading the list of things that went well, and a "Δ" (a triangle, the Greek letter delta and the mathematical symbol for change), heading the list of things that could be done differently (or changed) next time. This approach can be effective in identifying improvements for the next few meetings, but it requires a group in which all members are willing to speak freely about the group's performance, and it requires that time be allocated at the end of the meeting for discussion.

For a more detailed analysis, one which provides quantitative results that could show improvement over time, or in situations where group members may want to make their inputs anonymously, the group may want to consider a survey such as the one in Figure 16.2, with a basic five point scale from strongly agree to strongly disagree. A group may want to use a survey after a few meetings to get a sense of how things are going.

Use of a survey involves tabulating (although Web surveys can simplify this) and interpreting numerical scores. It's also important to determine in advance how the data will be used. Will there be an opportunity for written comments? Will the data be shared with the whole group? Will there be another survey in the future to look for improvement?

Figure 16.2—Sample Survey

Item	Response				
	Strongly Agree				Strongly Disagree
	5	4	3	2	1
1. Goals of the meeting were clear.					
2. Group members were prepared.					
3. All group members contributed effectively.					
4. Leadership was effective.					
5. Time was used effectively.					
6. Group accomplished goals.					
7. Next steps/activities are clear.					

SUMMARY

In summary, it is not difficult to manage a meeting effectively. It takes planning. It also requires one or more individuals at the meeting who can focus on the group process as well as the content of the meeting discussions, and maintain a broad view of the meeting's purpose and how it will be accomplished. If the group will be meeting regularly, there are tools for assessing and improving group meeting performance, to produce more satisfying meetings.

REFERENCES

Bens, Ingrid. (1999). *Facilitation at a Glance! Your Pocket Guide to Facilitation.* Cincinnati, OH: AQP and Participative Dynamics.

Burke, Dennis, et al. (2002). *Basic Facilitation Skills.* American Society for Quality, Human Leadership and Development Division; Association for Quality and Participation; International Association of Facilitators. Retrieved January 8, 2007 from http://www.iaf-world.org/i4a/pages/index.cfm?pageid=3387.

Chang, Richard Y. and Kevin R. Kehoe. (1993). *Meetings That Work!* Irvine, CA: Richard Chang Associates, Inc.

Doyle, Michael and David Straus. (1982). *How To Make Meetings Work.* New York, NY: Jove Books, Berkeley Publishing Group, Penguin Putnam, Inc.

GOAL/QPC-Oriel. (1995). *The Team Memory Jogger: A Pocket Guide for Team Members.* Madison, WI: Oriel.

Haynes, Marion E. (1988). *Effective Meeting Skills: A Practical Guide for More Productive Meetings.* Menlo Park, CA: Crisp Publications.

International Association of Facilitators. (1/9/07). http://www.iaf-world.org.

Kinlaw, Dennis C. (1993). *Team-Managed Facilitation: Critical Skills for Developing Self-Sufficient Teams.* San Diego, CA: Pfeiffer and Company.

Marshall, Jeanie. (1994). *Energetic Meetings: Enhancing Personal and Group Energy and Handling Difficult Behavior.* Santa Monica, CA: Jemel Publishing. http://www.mhmail.com.

Scholtes, P. R. et al. (1988). *The Team Handbook: How to Use Teams to Improve Quality.* Madison, WI: Joiner Associates Inc.

Townsend, John and Paul Donovan. (1999). *The Facilitator's Pocketbook.* Sterling, VA: Stylus Publishing, LLC.

Tannenbaum, Robert and Warren H. Schmidt. "How to Choose a Leadership Pattern," *Harvard Business Review*, Vol. 51 #3, May–June 1973, pp. 162–180.

VIRTUAL MEETINGS AND VIRTUAL TEAMS: USING TECHNOLOGY TO WORK SMARTER

You need to have a meeting. Some of the people you'd like to include are located at other campuses. All are eager to participate. But schedules and travel funds are so tight that none of the participants can find the time to travel to one location to meet face to face around a table.

You want to maximize the benefits of interaction and synergy while minimizing the resources needed to bring people together. You want all participants to be able to communicate at the same time, in real time, from different locations. You decide you'd like to use technology to schedule a "virtual" meeting, communicating without having to travel. What are your options, and what do you need to do to have a successful meeting?

This chapter discusses options for virtual meetings, suggests pointers for success, and provides resources for additional information. It's not a definitive review of options for holding a virtual meeting. This is a field in which the choices are continually evolving.

MEETING BASICS

First, the components of a successful traditional meeting still apply. Determine the purpose of the meeting you will be having: sharing information, generating ideas, evaluating options and making decisions, or assessing progress. Let participants know who will be attending the meeting. Develop an agenda and provide it to participants in advance, if possible, so all can be prepared. For each topic on the agenda, indicate who has the lead, and how much time you expect to spend on it. Identify someone to record the decisions made at the meeting, and afterwards promptly distribute minutes containing those decisions, next steps, action items, and individuals responsible, and a proposed agenda for the next meeting, if there will be one. If the group will have a series of meetings, have the group develop ground rules, so they know what to expect from each other. If there will be just one meeting, you can probably rely on common courtesies, such as not interrupting and being respectful of each other.

VIRTUAL MEETINGS

A virtual meeting adds a few more factors, since all at your meeting are not in the same room The first factor is related to preparation. You won't be able to hand out materials, so you'll need to plan how you will be providing all participants with any documentation. Fax or E-mail may be available, but you'll still need to allow some time for sending, receiving, and printing the documents. Make sure at the start of the meeting that all participants have all of the needed materials. You'll also need to make it clear during the meeting which document, and maybe even which page or section, is being referenced.

The most common concern about virtual meetings is the loss of non-verbal communication. Even if you can see the other participants on a video or PC screen, you may not be able to observe the finer points of body language. If you are in a chat room, you can't hear the tone of someone else's voice. However, there are also less obvious issues. You may not know for sure that your communication was received. You may not have any indication that others are listening. You may not be sure how long to wait for responses. These issues can be addressed by proactively discussing them at the start of your virtual session. They may also involve adding a section to your ground rules to specifically address issues related to a virtual meeting.

OPTIONS FOR VIRTUAL MEETINGS

You have several options for your meeting, and they are not all high-tech.

The easiest choice to start with is telephones for a *conference call.* Technical requirements are simple: you'll need a phone at each location, and a speaker phone if more than one person is at that location. You'll be able to hear each other, but you won't be able to see their face, body language, or how they are referring to written material.

If you'd like to see the other participants and their materials or documents, you can use *videoconferencing*. There are two approaches. The first is to meet in rooms equipped with dedicated videoconferencing equipment, including one or more monitor screens, camera(s), and a control system. The second is to meet via PC, for desktop video conferencing (DVC). For this, you'll need a camera, microphone, and speakers at each PC. Broadband connections will reduce delays in transmitting video images. There are tradeoffs of image quality, cost, access, and convenience between the two approaches.

A third alternative is *instant messaging* in a chat room via your PC. This is written, real time conversation via PC. A basic PC and Internet access is required. Some advance planning will be needed to determine the instant messaging provider you will be using and download their software, generally at no cost, to each meeting participant. Participants will use "buddy" names, and you may want to consider selecting names that will be easy for participants to associate with each individual.

If you do not need to meet at the same time, but need to exchange information, you have additional asynchronous options: fax, voice mail, E-mail, or an E-mail mailing list.

Finally, you have Web conferencing applications and Web groupware packages. Web conferencing uses a Web browser to allow you to share presentations over the Web in real time, and includes instant messaging. However, you may need to include a conference call for voice communications. Web groupware includes both synchronous tools (chat rooms and possibly voice or video via your PC) and asynchronous tools (shared space for document access and storage).

Additional Tips for Virtual Meetings

Consider the following points as you examine the options and decide how you can boost the input to your virtual meetings without increasing your time and cost for travel.

Planning your meeting

- Select your meeting medium: Look for a fit between the individuals in the group, the size of the group, the type of meeting, the meeting format, meeting length, and the technology available.
- Keep technology as simple as possible to meet your needs, so the technology doesn't interfere or compete with the content or flow of the meeting.
- Determine in advance what, if any, technical personnel support is needed and ensure that it will be available so your meeting can start on time.
- Have a back-up plan if there are technical difficulties (this may be as simple as being ready to switch to a conference call if there are PC difficulties).
- Distribute documents, allowing enough time for receipt and printing of documents, and make sure all are in hand at the start of the meeting.
- If you select an approach using your PC, use firewalls, antivirus software, and spyware protection, update your security tools, and keep your passwords secure. Do not give any personal or confidential information, especially when using your PC for a virtual meeting. Also comply with any additional PC security policies in your unit.

At the start of the meeting

- Begin with a face-to-face meeting whenever possible if subsequent meetings will be virtual.
- For a one-time virtual meeting, plan on introductions of all participants if required. For participants who know one another, a "Hello" from each person will allow everyone to know who is at the meeting.
- Consider a more formal opening, moderating, periodic summarizing, record keeping, and closing to keep the meeting on track and the participants aware of progress and decisions.

- Review with those attending any guidelines for the meeting, such as stating your name when you speak (if there are those who won't recognize each others' voices), and whether you plan to take a break during the meeting.
- Let the others know if you may have to leave the meeting early, or leave and return during the meeting.
- Consider providing some indicator to those in your work area that you are in a virtual meeting, not just working at your desk, and should not be interrupted.

During the meeting

- As the group leader or facilitator, consider creating more opportunities for remote participants to speak by specifically asking them if they have comments, so you don't fall into "out of sight, out of mind" low participation.
- In a chat room, consider using easily identifiable "buddy" names, and different colors and fonts for different individuals so you can quickly tell who's talking. Also, be ready to recognize multiple responses to one comment, and moderate the discussion so each response is addressed.

Asynchronous collaboration

- Ensure that all know and agree on the task, and when each step will be completed. Consider sending reminders, agreeing to send an announcement to all when a step is completed, or checking the central site for progress on a regular basis.

These pointers have been developed to provide you with the information you need to make the best use of technology in order to conduct successful meetings with satisfied participants. There are many ways to effectively use resources and technology to increase the exchange of information and discussion, and increase effectiveness and efficiency.

REFERENCES

Jude-York, D., Davis, L., and Wise, S. (2000). *Virtual Teaming: Breaking the Boundaries of Time and Place*. Menlo Park, CA: Crisp Publications.

Lipnack, J. and Stamps, J. (1997). *Virtual Teams: Reaching Across Space, Time, and Organizations with Technology*. New York, NY: John Wiley & Sons, Inc.

Mittelman, D. D., Briggs, R. O., Nunamaker, J. F. Jr. (1999). *Best Practices in Facilitating Virtual Meetings: Some Notes from Initial Experience*. Retrieved February 8, 2005 from http://mies.cs.depaul.edu/danny/GF.doc.

FACILITATING TEAMS FOR ORGANIZATIONAL IMPROVEMENT

This chapter focuses on the role of the facilitator in an improvement, innovation, project, or similar team. A project sponsor or team leader may wonder whether a project's scope warrants a facilitator at meetings. An individual may have been asked to facilitate a meeting and be uncertain about his or her role. Or a team leader may be trying to determine whether he or she can facilitate the process of a meeting and still manage the content of the discussions. While these are different perspectives, they all revolve around the role and responsibilities of a facilitator, and the dynamics of a group.

THE ROLE OF THE FACILITATOR

A team facilitator generally works with a team established to accomplish a specific task or project, not with an ongoing work team. The facilitator assists a team in determining where they are going and how they will get there. In most project management initiatives, the team knows what they need to implement, but the actual route to and through implementation has not been determined when the team starts work—that is the team's task. In innovation and improvement teams, the team is tasked with determining what innovations and improvements should be implemented to achieve an identified goal or outcome, as well as determining how their recommendations will be implemented.

Although they may use similar interactive approaches, the team facilitator differs from a facilitative trainer. A facilitative trainer knows where he or she expects the group to be at the end of the training session and knows what training objectives will be accomplished.

Activities within the team can be analyzed in terms of:

- Content—What the team is working on
- Process—How they are going about that work

Generally, team members focus on the content of the team activities, for example, how a unit can improve its internal information flow, or speed up response time for services. The team facilitator provides insight and guidance to the team leader and team members on team processes—how the team is dealing with or could deal with the specific content, tools the team could use such as surveys or focus groups, or how the team could set priorities or make the most effective decisions.

A team facilitator remains content neutral, and makes minimal content-related input to the group's discussions. This is to ensure that the team retains ownership for its decisions and recommendations. The team facilitator focuses on the group processes, ensuring that the team has access to the best available resources and tools.

The team facilitator collaborates with the:

- Team sponsor—the individual authorizing or charging the team, who controls resources and has the authority to implement changes
- Team leader—the individual administratively responsible for the team
- Team members—those with knowledge and interest in the initiative or project

Each contributes their knowledge, expertise, and relevant resources to accomplish the goal.

FACILITATOR RESPONSIBILITIES AND FUNCTIONS

The International Association of Facilitators' "Core Facilitator Competencies" provides one set of responsibilities and functions for a facilitator. This model addresses six areas—client relationships, group process, group participation, outcomes, facilitator development, and facilitator attitude—with several activities identified in each area.

1. **Create Collaborative Client Relationships**
   a. Develop working partnerships
   b. Design and customize applications to meet client needs
   c. Manage multi-session events effectively
2. **Plan Appropriate Group Processes**
   a. Select clear methods and processes
   b. Prepare time and space to support group processes
3. **Create and Sustain a Participatory Environment**
   a. Demonstrate effective participatory and interpersonal communication skills
   b. Honor and recognize diversity, ensuring inclusiveness
   c. Manage group conflict
   d. Evoke group creativity
4. **Guide Group to Appropriate and Useful Outcomes**
   a. Guide group with clear methods and processes
   b. Facilitate group self-awareness about its task
   c. Guide the group to consensus and desired outcomes
5. **Build and Maintain Professional Knowledge**
   a. Maintain a base of knowledge
   b. Know a range of facilitation methods
   c. Maintain professional standing
6. **Model Positive Professional Attitude**
   a. Practice self-assessment and self-awareness
   b. Act with integrity
   c. Trust group potential and model neutrality

Figure 18.1: Matrix of Facilitation

	One event requiring specific skills	Ongoing sessions requiring a broad range of skills
Joint: Working with team leader or meeting chair; mutual support and joint planning	Retreats	Planning, assessment, or innovation and improvement teams
Independent: Working alone with group; individually responsible to plan for expected and unexpected outcomes	Focus Groups	?

Given the competencies of a team facilitator, the first question to be addressed is what the client, sponsor, or team leader is asking the facilitator to facilitate. As shown in Figure 18.1, it may be a one-time event or ongoing team activities, and the facilitator may be working with a team leader or independently.

A retreat is an example of a one-time event in which the facilitator works with a team or work unit leader. A focus group is also a one-time event, but in this situation, the facilitator works independently, often to protect the confidentiality of individual inputs. Innovation, improvement, planning, or project teams meet repeatedly, and generally have a sponsor providing oversight as well as a leader attending meetings. The lower right quadrant of the matrix is populated with a "?" because it is difficult to imagine how a team facilitator could serve effectively working independently with a team on an ongoing basis. The organizational commitment to outcomes and implementation is difficult to identify in this scenario. The foundation of success in the first three examples, and what is missing in the fourth, is shared expectations between the facilitator and the team leader (or sponsor, project leader, or unit leader).

Prior to a facilitated session, the team leader and the facilitator must meet to discuss these expectations for the output and outcome, as well as the process. At this time they can determine what resources will be provided by whom to accomplish the desired outcomes. If the team leader will also be the facilitator, or is considering it, he/she needs to have this discussion with him/herself when planning the meeting.

In *Flawless Consulting,* Block presents a five-phase model for consulting that offers useful advice to both facilitators and team/project leaders. In the initial discussion, questions to be asked and answered include:

- What brought the team leader and facilitator together? What does the team leader want to have as an outcome?
- What is the facilitator capable of doing or providing?
- What support or commitment does the facilitator need from the team leader to ensure the desired outcome is reached?

Agreement should be reached on support, outcomes, and next steps. The facilitator will want to know that the team leader is willing to commit the time, the right people, and other necessary resources. The team leader will want assurance that the facilitator has the needed skills and knowledge. If the team leader will also be the facilitator, he/she will need to be confident in handling both sets of responsibilities.

Other issues to be initially discussed are confidentiality of group discussions, how to handle items such as safety or legal issues that cannot be kept confidential, and how to keep the leader informed of progress if he/she will not be attending the meetings.

The facilitator and team leader should consider a written agreement, essentially contracting with each other, although the contract may be as informal as an E-mail that summarizes what was agreed to at the planning meeting. In an improvement or project team, much of the information from this discussion may be included in the team's charter, the contract between the sponsor and the team.

Block points out that there may be situations in which the team leader is not willing to provide what the facilitator needs to ensure a successful event. Alternatively, the team leader may discover that the facilitator does not have the needed skills and knowledge. In those situations, the facilitator and team leader may not be able to reach agreement. This may also be the time when the team leader who is considering being the facilitator determines that having a neutral third party to manage the process may be helpful.

GROUP DYNAMICS

A facilitator needs to be aware of some basics of group dynamics and team development. These forces will be in play at the first meeting.

In 1965, Tuckman published what has become a classic model of group development. Since then, as shown in Figure 18.2, layers have been added to the model to provide more information about how the team and the team's facilitator are interacting.

It is important to note that while a team may have reached the performing stage, changes such as loss or addition of a member, loss of resources, or a change in schedule may move the team back to the storming stage. Also, since the team is working on a specific task or project, at some point they will come to a fifth stage of "adjourning."

FACILITATOR SKILLS AND TOOLS

One of the prime responsibilities of the facilitator is to assist the team in running effective, productive meetings. The team leader may spearhead the meetings (this is something to discuss in the contracting and planning stage), but it is up to the team facilitator to use his or her expertise to support the team leader. A facilitator assists with both group process and content, but should be cautious in maintaining content neutrality. How does the facilitator do this? First, he/she must ask the group a lot of questions and second, he/she must make observations, asking for clarification or confirmation.

The facilitator has a range of skills and tools to use in working with the team and dealing with the dynamics in the group. Since the role of the facilitator is to help an individual or team determine where they want to go and how to get there, it may not be surprising that some of the facilitator's skills are similar to those used in a counseling interaction between two people. These techniques, used in either a one-on-one situation or with a group, include:

- Attending behavior—relaxed, natural, eye contact, squared seating, comments that follow group discussion
- Invitation to talk—open-ended questions, non-evaluative
- Minimal encouragement to talk—use to keep discussion going

Figure 18.2—Stages of Team Development

Stage	Function	Feelings	Behaviors	Morale	Productivity	Facilitator level of activity
Form	Establish structure, roles, and plans for the team	- Excitement - Pride - Anxiety - Tentative team attachment	- Define task - Explore acceptable behavior - Abstract discussions - Complain about barriers	High	Low	High
Storm	Realization of and resistance to the amount of work that lies ahead	- Resistance to or changing attitudes about team - Concern - Tension	- Arguing - Defensiveness - Competition - Questioning - Disunity	Low	Starting to rise	High but decreasing
Norm	Acceptance of group norms, roles, and the CQI process	- Relief - Acceptance of team - Team cohesion - Can achieve goal	- Friendliness - Avoid conflict - Sharing - Establish ground rules	Rising	Rising	Decreasing
Perform	Work cohesively to achieve its goal of process improvement	- Understand each others' strengths and weaknesses - Satisfaction with progress - Attachment to team	- Constructive self-change - Work through problems - Maintain ground rules and boundaries	High	High	Low

Adapted from: B. Tuckman, "Development Sequence in Small Groups," *Psychological Bulletin*, 1965; R.B. Lacoursiere, *The Life Cycle of Groups: Group Developmental Stage Theory* (New York: Human Service Press, 1980); K. Blanchard, D. Carew, and E. Carew, *The One Minute Manager Builds High Performance Teams* (Blanchard Training and Development, Inc., Escondido, CA, 1990); P.R. Scholtes, et al, *The Team Handbook* (Joiner Associates, Madison, WI, 1996).

- Restatement or paraphrase—focus on content, check for understanding
- Reflection of feeling—address feelings in discussion
- Summarize—briefly restate content and feelings from a longer or extended discussion

Open-ended questions invite others to talk by starting with words such as who, when, and what. For example:

- Who else has a thought?
- Who has questions about that?
- What are some examples of that?
- Can anyone give some alternatives for that?

The key is to ask questions that cannot be answered with a "yes," "no," or one-word answer. Try to avoid "why" questions as they tend to put the respondent on the defensive, asking for justification. Minimal encouragement keeps the discussion going through brief responses from the facilitator such as "ok," "oh," "so," and "mmhmm," that show the facilitator is paying attention without interrupting the speaker. Questions such as "Can you tell me more about that?" are also in this category.

In restatement and paraphrasing, the facilitator is confirming that what he or she heard is what the speaker thought they said, by using different words or phrases to rephrase what the speaker said. It gives the speaker an opportunity to clarify what was said, and gives the facilitator and the rest of the group an opportunity to confirm what they heard. Reflecting feelings shows that the listener understands how excited or distressed the speaker was about the information they were relating. Active listening involves listening for both content and feelings.

Finally, the facilitator needs to be able to summarize the essence of discussions individuals or groups have had so that the team can identify the key points and decisions that need to be or have been made.

In a group setting, the facilitator may also be involved in:

- Initiating—get conversation going and keep it going by defining problems, suggesting procedures, proposing tasks, stimulating ideas

- Gate keeping—help to keep communication channels open, bring all into discussion, muffle dominant speakers, encourage non-contributors, ask for input
- Information and opinion seeking—draw out relevant information, opinions, suggestions from the group
- Clarifying and translating—ask for clarification, rephrase
- Mediating—defuse tension between opposing opinions or parties
- Testing consensus—check whether the group is really in agreement
- Encouraging—be friendly, warm, and responsive; use eye contact and verbal or non-verbal assurances

A facilitator can maintain order in the discussion by:

- Stacking—if several people want to speak at the same time, acknowledge all and establish order
- Tracking—if the facilitator hears multiple conversations or topics going on,
    - Tell the group
    - Identify and summarize each topic
    - Check with the group for accuracy on the topics
    - Help the group handle the topics one at a time
- Balancing—solicit other unexpressed views by asking "Does anyone have a different position?" or "What other thoughts does anyone have on this?" since silence does not always mean consent

While facilitating the discussion, listen for common ground:

- Tell the group if you are hearing differences and similarities
- Summarize differences
- Summarize similarities
- Check with the group for accuracy

One approach to facilitation is to make observations and statements and seek feedback, confirmation or disagreement. Another approach has the facilitator focus on asking questions. When taking the

Figure 18.3—The Ladder of Inference

Steps of the Ladder		**Facilitator Questions**
Decide whether and how to repond		What should I do?
Evaluate, interpret, and explain		What are the person's reasons for doing or saying this?
Translate and label		What does the data mean?
Select data		What am I paying attention to? Excluding?
Observe data		What do I observe?

Adapted from R. Schwarz, *The Skilled Facilitator* (Jossey-Bass, San Francisco, CA, 2002).

questioning approach, the facilitator needs to ensure that questions are not loaded or leading, set up to produce a desired or expected answer. The Ladder of Inference (see Figure 18.3) is one tool to use to avoid asking questions with hidden meanings.

The Ladder of Inference

Perceptions may be or become reality to the person who owns them. Throughout meetings a facilitator will observe many activities in a team, continually deciding whether, when, and how to intervene, respond, or react. The Ladder of Inference provides a way for a facilitator to check perceptions before acting on them. In the adaptation here from Schwarz's *The Skilled Facilitator*, when the facilitator finds him or herself on a level to the left (starting from the bottom), he or she should ask him or herself the questions on the right before proceeding up to the next step on the left. Asking the questions on the right can reduce the likelihood of making assumptions, coming to a wrong conclusion, and taking an inappropriate action.

Ground Rules

One tool for effective teamwork is ground rules. If the charter is the contract between the team and the team sponsor, ground rules are the contract team members make among themselves to clarify what they can expect from each other. In an ongoing situation, a facilitator may have the group develop their own ground rules. In a one-time event or for a specific task, so the group can focus on the task, the facilitator may bring a list of established ground rules and ask the group to agree to use them.

If the team develops its own ground rules, they are probably developed during the forming and storming stage; their development may be part of the team moving from storming to norming. By the time the team reaches the norming stage, ground rules should be understood, accepted, and followed. This is one of the reasons the role of the facilitator decreases as the team becomes more mature.

Ground rules generally include items that will be relevant at and through each meeting. This can include logistics items, such as starting and ending on time and sticking to the agenda. It can also include interpersonal items, such as listening to others, not interrupting, and not making long speeches.

Ground rules are also the place to address confidentiality and communication with others outside of the team. The team needs to find a balance that will make it possible to get input from or share progress with others but not contribute to rumors, and allow sensitive discussions or trial statements and ideas to remain within the team meetings.

There are short-term and long-term benefits to having ground rules. In the short term, they help the team make effective use of time and stay on track. In the longer term they help keep members on the team, because members' expectations for the team have been clarified up front, and they have had a role in determining how the team will operate.

Facilitating Team Content

In addition to managing group processes, the team facilitator assists the team leader with management of the content in the meetings, so that the team progresses toward its goal. These activities to gather and process content-related information will occur in parallel with the team's development, and can include:

- Initiating—Proposing tasks, defining problems, coordinating, clarifying, or suggesting an idea
- Giving information—Providing facts or information to assist the team in making a decision

- Energizing—Motivating the team to make a greater effort
- Evaluating or criticizing—Judging the evidence and conclusions the team suggests

To define and analyze the situation and alternatives, team members may take on the following roles, or the facilitator may ask the whole group to look at the issues from each of the following perspectives:

- Problem stater—clarifies, reminds of questions to answer
- Prober—seeks more information
- Devil's advocate—points out potential problems
- Idea generator—suggests creative solutions
- Model maker—suggests framework for analysis, completion, or new perspective
- Summarizer—points out apparent conclusions for verification and testing

Team content information probably comes from team members (since the facilitator is neutral on content), but the effective team facilitator may draw on different process tools and skills to bring the information out. The general approach is to gather as many ideas and alternatives as possible before the team begins to evaluate them. Once ideas are generated, the team can begin to prioritize them, or evaluate them in terms of established criteria, and narrow down the alternatives.

Remember that if the facilitator takes a position on content, he or she risks losing neutrality.

This can include not just offering content-related information, but also acknowledging inputs by using evaluative words such as "good."

CONFLICT AND CONSENSUS

Conflict can occur in teams due to difficult people, emotional issues, an individual's rank or status, multiple perspectives on an issue, or people who dominate the team through either the tone or quantity of their input to discussions.

Conflict is often thought of negatively. However, conflict is useful when it generates energy, leads to new ideas, leads to improvements, or leads to better understanding and unity. The alternative to conflict may be groupthink. In groupthink, team members are isolated, and reinforce and agree with each others' ideas without questioning or challenging. The outcome can be disastrous.

In *The Team Handbook,* Scholtes and others identify five classic responses to conflict:

- Avoiding—both the issues and the people
- Smoothing—minimize the conflict to maintain the relationship

  Actions of both avoiding and smoothing can include denying that there is a conflict, changing the topic to avoid the issue, or ignoring feelings about the issue; conflict continues out of sight.
- Forcing—use expertise, position, or other items to overpower others and force them to accept your position; increases likelihood of future conflict
- Compromising—look for outcome where everyone gains something, but also gives up something; may result in win-lose or lose-lose outcome
- Problem solving—look for win-win approach maintaining goals and relationships

In *Getting to Yes,* Fisher, Ury, and Patton point out that disagreeing individuals often quickly take adversarial positions which make discussion difficult or impossible. Shifting the discussion to their interests, what they desire as components or characteristics of the solution, may make discussion and resolution possible.

From the interpersonal perspective, guidelines to resolving conflict include:

- Avoid attacking the individual; preserve dignity and self respect
- Focus on the topic
- Stick to facts and data—be specific
- Listen with empathy and in the other person's shoes
- Express your perspective

Figure 18.4—Consensus Checklist

- Include everyone in the discussion
- Encourage expression of differences
- Clarify issues for understanding
- Promote open discussion of all ideas
- Avoid majority or minority rule voting
- Be wary of quick agreement
- Allow plenty of time
- Aim for a win-win scenario
- Place emphasis on understanding other points of view

- Ask questions and restate to clarify
- Look for areas of agreement
- Remember the common interests and goals
- Don't expect to change another's behavioral style

The goal from the facilitator's perspective is reaching consensus on significant decisions. Compromise is quicker than consensus, but will probably have less support from group members. Working for consensus and a win-win outcome can lead to synergy—the whole is greater than the sum of its parts and a team can produce better ideas than the same individuals working independently. In addition, reaching consensus will lead to stronger team member support of the decisions they have made.

In *Continuous Quality Improvement in Higher Education,* Dew and Nearing share the LUIS model used at Binghamton University to define and provide a means to reach an effective decision.

I can Live with this decision
I Understand this decision
I was Involved in this decision
I will Support this decision

All participants have been included on the team because they have useful contributions to make. It is the facilitator's job to create an environment that enables those contributions.

USING ALL AVAILABLE RESOURCES

The facilitator is a resource for process consultation, but is probably not the expert for all possible topics and issues. A facilitator should know when to call on other expert resources, and whom to contact. This may be particularly important regarding human resources, legal, or safety issues.

SUMMARY

When all aspects of facilitating a meeting are integrated into one process, the complete cycle of functions and activities of a team facilitator will include:

Before the meeting

- Planning
- Clarifying expectations and desired outcomes
- Identifying and obtaining resources

During the meeting

- Enabling the process
- Remaining neutral
- Maintaining group focus
- Dealing with conflict
- Enabling open communication, information sharing, problem solving, and decision making

After the meeting

- Providing feedback
- Planning for next steps
- Checking for follow through or scheduling a follow-up meeting

REFERENCES

Bens, Ingrid. (1999). *Facilitation at a Glance! Your Pocket Guide to Facilitation.* Cincinnati, OH: AQP and Participative Dynamics.

Block, Peter. (2000). *Flawless Consulting: A Guide to Getting Your Expertise Used.* San Francisco, CA: Jossey-Bass.

Brassard, M. (1989). *The Memory Jogger Plus +.* Methuen, MA: GOAL/QPC.

Burke, Dennis, et al. (2002). *Basic Facilitation Skills.* American Society for Quality, Human Leadership and Development Division; Association for Quality and Participation; International Association of Facilitators. Retrieved January 22, 2007 from http://www.iaf-world.org/i4a/pages/index.cfm?pageid=3387.

Dew, John and Molly Nearing. (2004). *Continuous Quality Improvement in Higher Education.* Westport, CT: American Council on Education/Praeger Series on Higher Education.

Doyle, Michael and David Straus. (1993). *How To Make Meetings Work.* New York, NY: Berkeley Publishing Group.

Fisher, Roger, William Ury, and Bruce Patton. (1991). *Getting to Yes: Negotiating Agreement Without Giving In.* New York, NY: Penguin Books.

GOAL/QPC-Oriel. (1995). *The Team Memory Jogger: A Pocket Guide for Team Members.* Madison, WI: Oriel.

International Association of Facilitators, http://www.iaf-world.org. Retrieved January 22, 2007.

International Association of Facilitators "Facilitator Competencies," *Group Facilitator: A Research and Application Journal,* 2000, (2) 2. retrieved May 28, 2009 from http://www.iaf-world.org/i4a/pages/Index.cfm?pageid=3331

Janis, Irving. (1982). *Groupthink: Psychological Studies of Policy Decisions and Fiascoes.* New York, NY: Houghton Mifflin Company.

Kinlaw, Dennis C., (1993). *Team-Managed Facilitation: Critical Skills for Developing Self-Sufficient Teams.* San Diego, CA: Pfeiffer and Company.

Kravitz, S. Michael. (1995). *Managing Negative People: Strategies for Success.* Menlo Park, CA: Crisp Publications.

Scholtes, Peter R. et al. (1996). *The Team Handbook (2nd Ed.).* Madison, WI: Joiner Associates Inc.

Scholtes, Peter R. (1998). *The Leader's Handbook.* New York, NY: McGraw-Hill.

Schwarz, Roger. (2002). *The Skilled Facilitator: A Comprehensive Resource for Consultants, Facilitators, Managers, Trainers, and Coaches.* San Francisco, CA: Jossey-Bass.

Townsend, John and Paul Donovan. (1999). *The Facilitator's Pocketbook.* Sterling, VA: Stylus Publishing, LLC.

TOOLS FOR ORGANIZATIONAL IMPROVEMENT

Penn State's IMPROVE model is a structured approach to facilitate problem solving, decision making, and process improvement teamwork. The model is an expansion of the Plan-Do-Check-Act model introduced by Walter Shewhart and popularized by W. Edwards Deming. This structured approach to teamwork has helped teams at Penn State to improve and redesign processes, programs, and services. Use of a common framework makes it easier to work together to share ideas.

This chapter presents an overview of many of the tools that can be used at different stages within the IMPROVE model. For each step in the IMPROVE model, some questions are included to help your team start the discussion. For each tool, this overview provides a brief statement of the purpose/function of the tool and how to use it.

Figure 19.1—Penn State's IMPROVE Model

I	Identify and Select Process for Improvement
M	Map the Critical Process
P	Prepare Analysis of Process Performance
R	Research and Develop Possible Solutions
O	Organize and Implement Improvement
V	Verify and Document Results
E	Evaluate and Plan for Continuous Improvement

Figure 19.2—IMPROVE Model Tools and Relational Issues

Stage	Goal	Data Tools[1]	Relational Issues[2]
I Identify and Select Process for Improvement	Establish a clear scope and purpose for the project	- Affinity diagram - Brainstorming - Check sheet - Is/is not analysis - Pareto chart - Stakeholder communication: surveys, interviews, and focus groups	- Establish a constructive group climate - Clarify roles, attendance expectations - Manage meetings effectively - Establish a shared understanding of the team's purpose
M Map the Critical Process	Clarify the current situation	- Flowchart or process map	- Establish norms for the constructive use of conflict communication and sensitivity to diversity issues - Create stakeholder communication plan
P Prepare Analysis of Process Performance	Assess process performance and analyze the cause of problems that are identified	- Histograms - Run charts/control charts - Fishbone diagram	- Reinforce buy-in for the use of structured communication tools to encourage critical thinking and avoid premature conclusions
R Research and Develop Possible Solutions	Propose, assess and prioritize potential solutions	- Benchmarking - Criteria matrix - Multivoting	- Reinforce equal participation and focused communication by assessing both the positive and negative aspects of potential solutions
O Organize and Implement Improvements	Plan and conduct the implementation of priority solutions	- Gantt chart - PERT chart - Responsibility matrix	- Address organizational change issues by planning for stakeholder communication and their involvement in the implementation - Clarify responsibility for implementation.
V Verify and Document Results	Assess the effectiveness of solutions	- Histograms - Run charts/control charts - Stakeholder communication	- Maintain team momentum through the elapsed time needed for implementation
E Evaluate and Plan for Continuous Improvement	Share lessons learned; anticipate future improvements	-Many of the above tools	- Stakeholder communication - Encourage closure by celebrating the team's success

[1] Tools are paired with stages but many can be used for more than one stage of the IMPROVE model.

[2] Many of the relational issues listed are present at more than one stage of the IMPROVE model. For more information, see *A Structured Approach to Organizational IMPROVEment.*

IDENTIFY AND SELECT PROCESS FOR IMPROVEMENT

Tools

- Affinity Diagram
- Brainstorming
- Check Sheet
- Is/Is Not Analysis
- Pareto Chart
- Stakeholder Communication: Surveys, Interviews, and Focus Groups

It is key that you select a process for improvement that will provide a return worthy of your team's effort. A thorough analysis at the start will ensure that your team's time will be well spent.

Definitions

Stakeholders. Those groups of people who have an interest in what your unit does; also those groups of people who have expectations about what your unit does.

Customers. A specific group of stakeholders, those who are the direct recipients or users of your products or services; may also be called clients, constituents, guests, or some other term.

Questions to start your team's discussion

- Whom do you serve? Who are your customers, clients, or constituents (internal or external)?
- What services or products do you provide to your customers, clients, or constituents? What do your products or services do or make possible for them?
- What do they expect of the services you provide?
- What processes are in place to meet or exceed those expectations?
- Who are your suppliers, those who provide input for your processes? What information do you provide to them? What information do they need from you?

- Who are your unit's other stakeholders? What do they expect? What information do you provide to them about your unit, and your products and services?
- Do you have information from your customers or co-workers that indicates that some of the processes are not meeting expectations?
- Which processes are within the scope of your unit's control?
- Which process will give you the most improvement for your effort?
- Is there a group of people who know enough to improve this process?
- Does your workplace welcome change?

Brainstorming

Generate new ideas among team members

- Clarify issue to be brainstormed
- Review guidelines for brainstorming:
  - No criticism, discussion, or evaluation
  - The more ideas the better
  - Be creative
  - Build on others' responses
  - Record all ideas for group to see
- Select type
  - Silent—each participant works individually for a few minutes; write each idea on one index card or sticky note; then share with the group, either round robin or through a facilitator
  - Round Robin—each participant shares one or a few (but not all) of their ideas; when all have had an opportunity to share, individuals can share more ideas
  - Spontaneous—all participants call out their ideas as they think of them; some participants may dominate the group
- Do it quickly
- Discuss only to clarify, not to critique

Check Sheet

Track the frequency of a particular event over time

Example

Goal: Reduce Interlibrary Loan (ILL) information phone calls by putting answers to most common questions on the Web

Data to be collected: Types of questions asked in phone calls

Is/Is Not Analysis

Sharpen the definition and scope of the issue at hand. Answer the following questions about the issue before the team:

- Who is/is not affected?
- What are/are not symptoms?
- When is the problem observed/not observed?
- Where does the problem occur/not occur?

Pareto Chart

Rank issues that have been identified from most significant to least, to determine which will yield the greatest return with improvement.

Stakeholder Communication

Surveys, Interviews, and Focus Groups. Collect additional data from stakeholders.

Survey. A questionnaire with standard questions; it may be written or someone may ask the questions and record the answers.

Interview. One individual asks another a set of questions, but may ask additional questions for clarification or additional detail as the interview progresses.

Focus group. A group of people guided by a moderator or facilitator in a discussion to provide information and feedback on a specific topic.

Figure 19.3—Summary of Data Collection Methods

Method or Tool	Description	Uses and Purposes
Check sheet	• form constructed and used to systematically record number of occurrences of an incident over time	• tally or compile data as collected • compile and summarize data from other methods
Interview (one-on-one)	• results-oriented discussions • vehicle for face-to-face communication with customer • interviewer asks questions, encourages, and actively listens to customer responses	• collect information from customers, especially qualitative data • establish relationship with customers • initial or preliminary data-gathering • test wording or focus of written questionnaire
Group Interview or Focus Group	• group interview led by a facilitator or moderator • occasionally recorded with audio or videotape if permission is granted	• collect information from customers • obtain constructive criticism • pilot questionnaires • establish relationship with and among participants
Electronic Focus Group	• computer network co-facilitated by group facilitator and computer software expert	• anonymous input—more open, more input • computer aids in analysis
Written Survey	• printed questionnaire requiring written responses • may be modified for use by mail, e-mail, phone, individual interviews or focus groups	• to reach large number of respondents
Historical Data	• data previously collected	• analyze data for related occurrences, events linked over time, patterns which define a group, or future value of a data item

Figure 19.3—Summary of Data Collection Methods

Method or Tool	Potential Advantages	Potential Disadvantages or Problems
Check sheet	• simplicity • no computer required	• not interactive
Interview (one-on-one)	• open lines of communication • build relationships • opportunity to clarify and expand on questions of importance to interviewee • less work for interviewee	• can be inefficient or unproductive if not carefully structured • interviewer differences • lack of anonymity • time consuming for interviewers • works best for small number of interviewees
Group Interview or Focus Group	• more information than in interview due to group interaction • clarification possible • synergism—new ideas • less time invested than with individual interviews	• difficult to moderate—requires more skill from discussion leader • susceptible to moderator or group bias • reliability and validity often questioned • lack of anonymity • groupthink
Electronic Focus Group	• less time required • can reduce travel if done at remote locations	• more pre-session planning • additional expense for facility/equipment and computer expert
Written Survey	• greater number of responses expected • preserves anonymity	• less chance to clarify or expand on questions and answers • low response rate may affect representative features
Historical Data	• data have already been collected and are available	• need to reformat data or develop specific queries

MAP THE PROCESS

Tools

- Flowchart (traditional and top down); also known as a Process Map

One of the key pieces of data in your improvement initiative is documentation of the current process. This should lead to understanding among all team members of that process, and represent all the steps in that process of which team members have knowledge.

Definition

Process. A sequence of steps to respond to a request or use resources (time, information, material, etc.) to produce and deliver the service or product a unit provides.

Questions to start your team's discussion

- What are the steps you go through as you provide your product or service?
- What is the sequence of steps from the time you receive a request or start a process to the time you deliver your product or service to your client?
- How do you respond to missing or incorrect material or information?
- Are there times between the steps when nothing is happening? How long and frequent are these "wait" states?

Flowchart/Process Map

Traditional Flowchart Symbols

Start/Stop

Process step

Decision step

Wait state

Direction of flow

Represent the steps in a process or procedure graphically:

Steps to develop a <u>flowchart/process map</u>	**<u>Pointers</u>**
1. Identify boundaries	Starting and ending point All steps between represented on the team/at the table
2. Determine level of detail	Macro or micro
3. List major steps	Show what actually is, not the ideal or theoretical Arrange in sequence
4. Draw a diagram	Symbols Arrows Only one arrow out of a process No endless loops No dead ends
5. Review	Accuracy Consensus
6. Label	Title Date

PREPARE ANALYSIS OF PROCESS PERFORMANCE

Tools

- Histograms
- Run Charts
- Control Charts
- Fishbone Diagram

In this stage, you are identifying a way to measure a unit's performance (and the improvement of that performance), and gathering baseline data of those measurements. You are also looking for the 'root causes' of any unsatisfactory performance.

Definitions

Data. A way of measuring a unit's performance, and improvement of that performance.

Root cause. The underlying, fundamental cause of a process performance problem. When you identify the root cause and make improvements to address it, the problem will be solved and will not resurface elsewhere.

Questions to start your team's discussion

- What data would you like to have about your work unit's performance to know how well you are meeting stakeholders' expectations?
- What change in those measures would indicate improvement?
- In choosing a product or service, what are specific client, supplier, and other stakeholder *expectations* for your product or service?
    - What do clients, suppliers, and other stakeholders realistically expect with regard to your product or service?
    - Ideally, what would clients, suppliers, and other stakeholders like to see in your product or service?
- What are specific client, supplier, and other stakeholder *satisfaction or performance measures* regarding their *expectations* for *your* product or service? For example:
    - Quality
    - Courtesy in dealing with them
    - Cost
    - Sharing of status information
    - Time from order to delivery
    - Error rate

Example

Over 10 days, you have asked those picking up Interlibrary Loan books to complete a satisfaction survey. The data is shown in the table. You counted the occurrence of a particular event each day, in this case the number of dissatisfied clients. You decided to use the tools below to analyze your data.

Day	Number of Dissatisfied Clients (Events)
1	15
2	19
3	15
4	25
5	17
6	10
7	8
8	13
9	12
10	15

Histogram. Display a summary of the frequency of occurrences; a vertical bar chart.

1. List your data points in increasing order.
2. Identify the lowest and highest value data point.
3. Subtract the lowest value from the highest to determine the range of your data.
4. Divide this range into an odd number of equally sized categories (known as 'classes'). The key is to have categories/ classes of equal size, and have each data point fit in only one category. You can create these categories manually, starting with your lowest value (or a value close to it) and adding the same amount (approximately equal to your range divided by the number of categories) until you have included your largest value. Mark these categories on the x (horizontal) axis.
5. Count the number of data points in each category or class, and mark the y (vertical) axis with values to reflect the smallest to largest number of data points in the categories.
6. For each category on the x axis, draw a bar to reflect the number of data points in that category

For more information on constructing histograms and calculating classes, see Brassard and Ritter, *The Memory Jogger II*.

Run Chart. Display performance over time to identify trends, patterns, and variations; a line graph.

1. List your data points in chronological (time, day, month, etc.) order.
2. Set up the x (horizontal) axis to reflect chronological points (time, day, etc.).
3. Set up the y (vertical) axis to reflect the range of values of the data points.
4. For each chronological point on the x axis, plot the value of the data point for that time or day on the y axis.

Control Chart. Display of performance over time (run chart) that also contains upper and lower boundaries of expected performance, based on past performance, within the system. The type of control chart you construct will be determined by the type of data (attribute, such as number of errors, or variable, such as length of time) and type of sample (fixed size or changeable). For more information on the different types of control charts and how to construct them, see Brassard and Ritter, *The Memory Jogger II*.

Fishbone Diagram. A graphic display of categories of causes that could be leading to a particular result or effect; relationship among the causes of the problem. Also known as a *Cause and Effect* or *Ishikawa* diagram, or the *Five Whys* approach.

RESEARCH AND DEVELOP POSSIBLE SOLUTIONS

Tools

- Benchmarking
- Criteria Matrix
- Multivoting

Your team should be able to identify more than one possible way to improve the process you are working on. The key, once you have identified several possible options, is to evaluate and select the most effective combination of options to arrive at the solution.

Questions to start your team's discussion

1. Identifying possible solutions
    - Is information missing or incorrect?
    - Are there unnecessary steps?
    - Does each step add value to the process?
    - Are any steps duplicated?
    - Are steps in logical sequence?
    - Are there unnecessary layers of approval?
    - Are there overlapping paper and electronic processes?
    - Is all paperwork necessary?
    - Are multiple people responsible for the same task?
    - Does the process take too much time?
    - Can you reduce wait time?
    - Do unnecessary complications or delays exist?
    - Where are the bottlenecks—places where everything backs up or slows down?
    - Is there rework being done?
    - Can you provide a new or better product or service?

You may have answered some of these questions when you developed your baseline flowchart. Improvements and innovations that are identified and implemented early in the analysis are called "low hanging fruit."

2. Evaluating your possible solutions
    - What are the potential benefits of the solutions?
    - What could go wrong with the solutions?
    - What are the projected costs?
    - Have you gathered ideas from others involved in the process about how it can be improved?
    - Are the solutions based on what you have learned?
    - Do the solutions address the causes?
    - Have you thought about eliminating or redesigning some of the steps in the process?

- Have you identified ways to try out each solution?
- Will the improvement address customer concerns?

Benchmarking. Compare your processes, procedures, services, and products to similar ones at highly successful organizations.

Data sources include:

- Existing Public Information: Television, newspapers, trade journals; internal experts and studies; conferences and seminars; external experts
- New Information: Searches and original research
- Personal Contact: Meet with organizational representatives and exchange information

Organizational sources include:

- Internal: Compare with similar units in your organization
- Competitors: Compare with similar organizations in the same industry
- Functional: Compare with different organizations in other fields performing the same function
- Generic: compare to an organization with a process that has a similar activity

Criteria Matrix. The criteria matrix can be used to systematically evaluate alternatives and determine their relative feasibility. First, review all the constraints and criteria for the solution and develop a list of required and desired criteria. These criteria can include more tangible items such as cost, time to complete, and whether a deadline can be met, as well as less tangible items such as allowing for user feedback. Then evaluate each alternative solution on each of the criteria, using a 0 to 10 scale or another approach. Total the points for each alternative. The alternative with the highest score is the one that will best meet the criteria.

Multivoting. Prioritize or rank ideas.

1. Follow brainstorming procedure.
2. Examine posted ideas and combine similar items.

3. Assign each member a number of "votes" (often one third of the total number of items to be voted upon).
4. Members assign their votes to their preferred items; group can decide whether to allow only one vote per item, or allow multiple votes to be cast for one item.
5. Select items with the most votes.

If necessary, repeat steps three to five to narrow the list to a manageable number for further consideration.

ORGANIZE AND IMPLEMENT IMPROVEMENTS

Tools

- Gantt Chart
- PERT Chart
- Responsibility Matrix

Once recommendations are accepted by those with the resources and responsibility to implement them, a plan for this implementation must be developed and executed. Essentially, the improvement project needs to be managed.

Definition

Project Management. A means to identify and commit resources (time, money, people, facilities, etc.) to achieve an outcome within budget, on time, and within standards.

Questions to start your team's discussion

- What steps need to be taken to implement the solutions and how long will they take?
- Is there leadership support to move forward?
- Are additional resources (e.g., money, staff, equipment) needed?
- Is training needed?

- Have the persons responsible for implementing the change given input about potential roadblocks or barriers, or factors that will facilitate the implementation?
- Has a communication plan been developed to inform all the stakeholders about the proposed changes in the process?
- What is the plan for monitoring the process once the change has been implemented?

Example

Use a Gantt chart and PERT chart to plan for increasing enrollment in CQI programs through presentations to unit heads.

Gantt Chart. A horizontal bar chart; shows concurrent and sequential tasks with minimum time for project.

PERT (Program Evaluation and Review Technique) Chart. A graphic showing the critical path, the longest path with essential steps; for projects with many interactive steps.

Responsibility Matrix. Assign responsibilities and set target dates for completion

VERIFY AND DOCUMENT RESULTS

Tools

- Histograms
- Run Charts/Control Charts
- Stakeholder Communication: Surveys, Focus Groups, and Interviews

Repeat the pre-improvement data collection to provide information for an "after" assessment to compare with the "before." Use this to design the next iteration or implement the pilot systemwide. Also use this data to share the information about your team's accomplishments.

Questions to start your team's discussion

- How does the comparison of the before and after data fit with your expectations? Where are your expectations met? Where are they not met?
- Where are the areas that the improvement needs fine tuning?
- What do you need to do to roll out the improvement in a larger area or system-wide?
- How can you effectively share this information about improvement and innovation?

EVALUATE AND PLAN FOR CONTINUOUS IMPROVEMENT

Tools

- Many of the previously listed tools

The opportunities for improvement don't end once your process has been improved. Change is continuous and improvement needs to be continuous as well.

Questions to start your team's discussion

- Now that you have a solution in place, how do you continue to evaluate and improve your process?
- Where are there other areas for improvement?
- What lessons have been learned about process improvement?
- How can you continue to utilize the skills developed by the team members?

RESOURCES

Examples of the tools described in this chapter may be found at http://www.psu.edu/president/pia/books/.

REFERENCES

Bens, I. (1999). *Facilitation at a Glance—A Pocket Guide of Tools & Techniques for Effective Meeting Facilitation*. Association of Quality & Participation/Participation Dynamics.

Brassard, M. (1989). *The Memory Jogger Plus +*. Methuen, MA: GOAL/QPC.

Brassard, M. and D. Ritter. (1994). *The Memory Jogger II: A Pocket Guide of Tools for Continuous Improvement & Effective Planning*. Methuen, MA: GOAL/QPC.

Goal/QPC-Oriel, Inc. (1995). *The Team Memory Jogger: A Pocket Guide for Team Members*. Madison, WI: Oriel.

Scholtes, P. R, Joiner, B., & B. Streibel (1996). *The Team Handbook: How to Use Teams to Improve Quality 2nd ed.* Madison, WI: Joiner Associates Inc.

Scholtes, P.R. (1998). *The Leader's Handbook*. New York, NY: McGraw-Hill.

USING SURVEYS FOR DATA COLLECTION IN CONTINUOUS IMPROVEMENT

An integral part of a well-designed survey is to "plan in" quality all along the way. One must devise ways to keep respondent mistakes and biases to a minimum.

Scheuren, 2004 (p. 18)

Data-based decision making, an essential element of Continuous Quality Improvement (CQI), helps individuals and teams to assess the efficiency and effectiveness of current processes. Numerous methods exist for collecting data. Focus groups, personal interviews, surveys, review of internal records, and counting events are some methods to gather data. This chapter explains how to use surveys to obtain data.

WHAT IS A SURVEY?

A survey is a research method for collecting information from a selected group of people using standardized questionnaires or interviews. While many people think of a questionnaire as the survey, the questionnaire is just one part of the survey process. Surveys also require selecting populations for inclusion, pre-testing instruments, determining delivery methods, ensuring validity, and analyzing results.

In Continuous Quality Improvement, surveys help to identify customer expectations, measure satisfaction levels, and determine specific areas for improvement.

IS A SURVEY NECESSARY?

Surveys that provide valid, usable results require thought, planning, logistical support, time and possibly, money. Consider first whether the data are available from other data sources or collection methods. For example,

- Rather than asking employees how many times they used a certain service, check records.
- To determine the number of students using tutoring services, sign-in sheets could be located at each area.

Other sources of information might include published reports, previous surveys of students, staff, or faculty, and other internal data or records.

Richard Light, a nationally recognized proponent of conducting and using research, especially in the area of student assessment, believes that good research is one of the most important bases for sound decision making. Light and colleagues (1990) have argued that, "If used wisely, it [survey research] can lead to improvements throughout the entire fabric of an institution" (p. 234).

At the same time, they caution would-be data gatherers to think carefully before adding to the mountain of unused and often unusable survey data. Serious, targeted, and well-directed surveys that are sensibly integrated into an overall assessment and improvement approach can be a valuable tool, but individuals who are planning a survey should "weigh the costs against the benefits" (p. 10). Teams should not embark on a survey simply because it seems like the thing to do. A useful question to keep in mind is, "What do you want to come out of this?" (p. 232).

If no other data source is available, then a survey may be necessary.

INITIAL DECISIONS

To be useful in Continuous Quality Improvement, survey results must be valid, that is, the survey must measure what it intends to measure. Validity depends on how much error enters into a survey process. Some possible sources of error are:

- whether the people surveyed represent the true population under study;

- how well the respondents understood the questions asked;
- how willing people are to participate in the survey process; and,
- how well the results are analyzed.

To avoid errors like these, a team undertaking a survey needs to consider several basic questions at the start.

How will the survey results be used?

The purpose of the survey drives the collection method, the persons to be included in the survey process, the types of questions asked, and many other factors. The goal of the survey should be to collect objective, unbiased information from a representative group of stakeholders. One helpful step to take up front is to outline what you want to learn from the survey and how the results will help the team improve their processes. The survey should focus on the improvement of processes rather than individuals.

Who should be surveyed?

One way to increase validity of survey results is to ensure that participants in the survey process are the stakeholders who are affected by or involved in the processes under review in the survey. These persons will be the ones most knowledgeable about the outcomes and impacts of the process and have the most relevant input for improvement.

How many should be surveyed?

Some surveys include all people within a population, while others sample just a subset of these individuals. Sampling, if done correctly, lowers the costs of surveys and decreases the logistics involved. For paper questionnaires, it decreases the costs of printing and mailing questionnaires and saves time required for entering data. Sampling also burdens fewer persons with completing a questionnaire or participating in an interview.

Who will design and administer the questionnaire and analyze the results?

Part of the answer to this question depends on how much time, money, expertise, and personnel resources are available. Survey administration requires a commitment of personnel time in developing the questionnaire, sending out questionnaires, following up with non-respondents, processing and entering data, and analyzing results. Preparation, administration, and analysis of a questionnaire takes time and may be better handled by a company outside of the organization. In addition, questionnaires that include sensitive topics might be better administered by an outside organization. Recipients may be more willing to respond to what they perceive as a more neutral or objective party.

It is crucial that the people most involved with the processes under study, and the people using the results of the survey be included in the team that develops the questions. They have the most knowledge of the process and how the results will be used.

Do we need to submit an application to the Institutional Review Board?

Typically, many surveys conducted by quality improvement teams are not considered research since the results are kept internal to the institution and do not add to "generalizable knowledge."

SURVEY FORMAT

Surveys can be conducted through:

- face-to-face interviews
- telephone interviews
- paper questionnaires
- online questionnaires
- a combination of these methods

Some factors to consider in deciding on a format are:

Cost. The cost of face-to-face and telephone interviews are generally higher than other formats and stem from interviewer expenses.

Paper survey costs depend on the material, printing, and postage costs. The cost of an electronic format survey depends on whether software is purchased or a free online survey service is used. Several companies offer limited Web survey services at no cost. (These types of services can be found by using a Web search engine to search for "free Web surveys.") Generally, Web surveys tend to be the least expensive format.

Project Length. Across all survey formats, development of the questionnaire generally will take about the same amount of time. Administration of the questionnaire and the data entry requirements vary by format. Typically, online questionnaires require the least amount of time because the delivery is almost instantaneous and the time required for data entry is short.

Sampling Bias. To provide valid and useful results, the population being surveyed should fairly represent stakeholders. Some survey formats, such as online surveys, may not reach a fair representation of the audience since some members may not have access to the Web or E-mail. For example, since older people are less likely to use the Internet and E-mail, an online survey of retired persons may not be the best choice. A mailed or phone survey may be a better choice for these types of audiences.

DEVELOPING A QUESTIONNAIRE

Basic questionnaires consist of a cover letter, the questionnaire, and a concluding page. The cover letter should be brief and appear at the front of the questionnaire. This cover letter should address:

- the purpose of the survey
- the persons conducting the survey
- the date by which the form should be returned
- an estimate of the time required for completion
- the confidentiality policy
- a person to contact

The goal of writing a survey question for self-administration is to develop a query that every potential respondent will interpret in the same way, be able to respond to accurately, and be willing to answer.

Dillman, 2000 (p.32)

After completing the questions, respondents should be thanked for their participation and should again be given the name of a person to contact in case they have questions about the survey.

TYPES OF SURVEY QUESTIONS

Questions fall into two categories: open-ended and closed. In *open-ended questions*, participants answer the questions in their own words. These types of questions are useful in eliciting respondent feelings, and to provide depth to an issue. They should be written in a manner that precludes one-word responses, such as "Yes" or "No."

Instead of asking:
"Are you satisfied with this service? "
Ask:
"With what aspects of this service are you satisfied?"

Open-ended questions provide much information about the selected topics, but they are more difficult to analyze since they may cover a wide range of topics and need to be coded or grouped to provide some level of summary.

Closed questions provide the respondent with a defined set of answers. The response set can include categorical or scaled responses. Categorical question response sets have no inherent ordering within them. A question about gender is categorical (Male, Female), as is a question about type of transportation to work (car, bus, taxi, bicycle, walk).

Scaled responses, on the other hand, have some type of progressive order. A question about age is one example of a scaled question while another is a question that asks respondents to rate their agreement or satisfaction. Although responses to the latter may not have a numerical value (i.e., Very Satisfied, Somewhat Satisfied, Neutral, etc.), they are scaled because they have a progressive order.

WRITING QUESTIONS

Generally, even if an outside resource administers the survey process, individuals on the teams who are working on the process improvement are the ones to identify the topics and types of questions to be included. The following suggestions can help lessen survey error because they focus on increasing question clarity and participant motivation to complete questions:

Begin the questionnaire with simple questions. Ease respondents into completing the form by asking simple questions that are not open-ended. This may make respondents more comfortable and they may be more likely to complete the questionnaire. However, the initial questions should also be sufficiently interesting to the respondent to attract their attention and make them want to complete the survey. Thus, questions about demographic information, such as gender or age, should not be the first questions on the page, even though they are straightforward.

Use concise sentences. Keep the questions as short as possible, but provide enough context that respondents can understand the question.

Use words and language that respondents will understand. Many experts recommend writing questions at the eighth-grade level. Dillman (2000, p.52) suggests "When a word exceeds six or seven letters, chances are that a shorter and more easily understood word can be substituted" and gives the example of using the word "tired" rather than "exhausted." Also avoid words, expressions, or acronyms that are unique to a specific department, discipline, or area.

Ask only one item per question. Focus the question on one action or attribute only. For example, "How satisfied are you with the knowledge and courtesy of our staff?" asks the respondent to rate staff on both their knowledge and manners, two different traits. Staff may be knowledgeable, but not courteous, and responses would not reflect a discrepancy between the two.

Provide balance in responses. To prevent bias, an equal number of positive and negative responses should be offered in a question and the responses at each end of the scale should be the same in weight. For instance, if "Very Satisfied" appears at one end of a scaled range, the choice on the other end should be "Very Dissatisfied," not "Terribly Dissatisfied."

Offer neutral response as a choice. Questions that ask respondents to rate an area should include a "Neutral" response category.

Offer "not applicable" or "does not apply" as a choice. Including one of these two choices as an option is important for two reasons. First, respondents who have no knowledge of or experience with the question topic should not assess or comment on it. Second, the respondents who choose "not applicable" reflect any subgroups that do not use a service. This can provide a measure of the true usage of a service or process.

Use a natural flow for questions. The flow of the questions should be logical: Question 3 should follow Question 2, while Question 4 should follow Question 3. If possible, avoid asking the respondent to skip questions, especially on paper questionnaires, since it can confuse respondents. Online forms, however, can unobtrusively target questions to specific groups by automatic flowing. Many Web survey packages allow questions to flow based on the categories respondents select in previous questions.

Create categories that cover all possible responses and are mutually exclusive. The responses for each question should cover all possible alternatives and should not overlap. For example, Columns A and B below show response categories to a question which asks students about the amount of time they study per day.

Column A	Column B
a) 0 hours	a) 0 hours
b) 1-2 hours	b) Less than 1 hour
c) 2-3 hours	c) At least 1 but less than 3 hours
d) 3-4 hours	d) At least 3 but less than 5 hours
e) 4 or more hours	e) 5 or more hours

Under Column A, a student who studied for 45 minutes a day would not be able to select a correct response, while a student studying 3 hours a day could select c) or d). Column B displays preferable categories which cover all possible hours yet do not overlap.

Include plenty of space for written comments. Encourage respondents to write more by providing an adequate number of lines for responses. More lines may prompt respondents to write longer answers.

Prompt respondents with specific time frames. Providing a common reference point increases the likelihood that respondents will understand questions in a similar manner. Mentions of time may also help participants to better remember their actual activities.

> Instead of asking:
> "How often do you travel outside Pennsylvania?"
> Ask:
> "Since January 2006, how often have you traveled outside of Pennsylvania?"

Keep the questionnaire as short as possible. Response rate has a great impact on survey validity and minimizing questionnaire length increases response rates. Respondents to long questionnaires more frequently skip over questions, adding to non-response errors for individual questions. In creating questionnaires, developers should include those questions that are "must-haves" and reconsider those that are "nice-to-haves."

Minimize identifying questions. Respondents feel more comfortable if they believe they can not be identified from their responses, and are more likely to complete questionnaires. For example, if the population under study includes few females over the age of 50, older women may be less likely to complete the questionnaire because their individual responses could be identified. It may be important for the team to know the composition of the respondents and whether certain groups have different experiences, but to increase response rates, keep demographic questions to a minimum.

Be consistent in question wording when looking at trends. To accurately assess changes over time, the same questions that appeared on past questionnaires should be used. If the questions vary, apparent differences could be due to measurement issues and not reflect an actual change.

PRE-TESTING THE QUESTIONNAIRE

Prior to distributing the questionnaire, many survey researchers recommend recruiting a small group to complete the questionnaire and provide input on their understanding of the questions and ability to complete it. The group can include as few as five to ten people. Items to cover with the persons pre-testing the questionnaire include: 1) any terms or words that were unfamiliar; 2) the clarity of the questions; 3) the flow of the questionnaire; 4) ability to access the form if online; and, 5) the actual time required to complete the questionnaire. Team members can sit with the participants as they complete the pre-test, can personally interview or survey each participant after she or he completes the pre-test, or can hold focus groups with the participants after they complete the pre-test. This type of feedback can improve the quality of the questionnaire.

INCREASING RESPONSE RATES

Dillman (2000) recommends making five contacts with participants in order to increase response rates for mailed and online surveys. His research, along with that of others, has found that increasing the number of contacts can have a significant effect on return rates, thus increasing survey validity.

- The first contact occurs a few days prior to distributing the questionnaire and informs the participant that they will receive a questionnaire shortly.
- The participant receives the questionnaire two to three days later. Dillman recommends placing an identification code on each questionnaire so that responses can be tracked.
- Three days to a week later, the participant receives a thank you postcard. The note thanks participants for completing and returning the survey, and asks that persons who have not already completed survey to do so.
- The fourth contact occurs two to four weeks after the initial questionnaire. It consists of a replacement questionnaire sent to those persons who have not yet responded.

- About a week after the fourth contact, Dillman recommends that a fifth contact be made through a delivery method that differs from the initial contacts, i.e., a phone call if the others were by E-mail, or a priority postal mailing if the others were sent by general delivery.

Using Dillman's guidelines, from the time the pre-notice is sent to the time all completed questionnaires are received requires about two months. Other strategies which have been shown to increase response rates include personalizing all correspondence or including token financial or other incentives.

DATA TABULATION

After all questionnaires are received, the results are tabulated. For very simple surveys, the results may be hand-tallied and the responses to each category for every question are counted. This approach is manageable only if the number of respondents is very small and the questions are limited.

Most surveys are more complex and require construction of a database. For paper formats and interviews, this means that responses to each question are entered into some type of data file for analysis. (Web surveys have the advantage here of having each respondent's answers automatically entered into a data file, thus saving on data entry time.) Spreadsheet, database, and statistical analysis software is available for this step. Whatever software is used, the data entered should be double-checked for data entry errors.

Once the results are tabulated by hand or in a database, the composition of the respondents should be compared to the composition of the entire population that received the survey. Characteristics for this type of comparison include information such as gender, staff/faculty status, years employed, or work unit. This step indicates whether the respondents to the questionnaire are representative of the entire group. Discrepancies between the two groups need to be noted in the results; substantial differences limit the team's ability to generalize the results.

CALCULATING DESCRIPTIVE STATISTICS

Simple descriptive statistics such as frequency counts and percentage distributions provide the basic information teams need to answer the questions for which they initially started the survey process.

Frequency counts provide the number of respondents who selected each category in a question. For example as shown in the table below, 100 persons were included in each of two separate surveys. In Survey A, 40 persons responded "Yes" and 30 persons did so in Survey B. The counts for all other response categories also appear in the tables.

EXAMPLE: Were you satisfied with the quality of the service you received during your last appointment?

SURVEY A			
Response	# of Responses	% of Total Responses	% of Responses (Not Including NA)
Yes	40	40%	50%
No	40	40%	50%
Not Applicable	20	20%	-----
TOTAL	100	100%	100%
SURVEY B			
Response	# of Responses	% of Total Responses	% of Responses (Not Including NA)
Yes	30	30%	50%
No	30	30%	50%
Not Applicable	40	40%	------
TOTAL	100	100%	100%

In addition to the frequencies, *percentage distributions* are useful, and should be calculated in a manner that reflects the data appropriately. The percentage distribution is the number of responses in each category divided by the total number of responses. For instance, 40 percent (40/100) of the persons in Survey A and 30 (30/100) percent in Survey B responded "Yes." This is the straight percentage response.

The team should decide whether the percentage distributions based on the total number of responses is sufficient or whether the distribution should be based on the number of *valid responses*. Typically, valid responses exclude the categories of missing and "Not Applicable" responses. The calculation is shown in the last column in the table above.

It is important to know how many persons selected each response, but "Not Applicable," along with missing responses, may need to be excluded from calculations of percentage distributions which are used for comparisons. For example, 20 persons in Survey A felt the question was not applicable as did 40 persons in Survey B. Excluding the "Not Applicable" responses shows that half of the respondents in both Survey A (40/80) and Survey B (30/60) responded "Yes." Analyzing responses only for those persons who use a service better reflects true satisfaction levels.

ANALYSIS OF RESULTS

Once the frequency tables and percentage distributions are available, team members can begin to analyze the data. One way to do this is to look for patterns within the data. Some specific areas include:

Comparison within a survey. Response patterns for certain questions may stand out from the others and may indicate an area for improvement. For example, 20 percent of respondents may be satisfied with the waiting time for a process while 60 percent may have reported they were satisfied with the quality of the process. Because of the relatively low satisfaction level with wait time, the team may identify this as an area for improvement.

Comparison across subgroups. Breaking out questionnaire responses by specific characteristics helps teams determine whether certain groups have different experiences. For example, employees who work on a part-time basis may rate availability of parking lower than employees who work full-time. Analysis of group differences depends on the types of attributes captured in the survey, for example, gender, employment status, or department.

Comparison across time. Comparisons across time are typically made to determine whether implemented process improvements are having the desired effect, and also to identify areas with declining performance or satisfaction for process improvement. The questions and sampling population need to be the same across both surveys to ensure that the apparent change is an actual change and not the result of differences in measurement.

Comparison with specific goals. Some teams may be working with processes that have established goals. In addition, teams may want to benchmark with other areas within the institution or other institutions. Similar to comparisons across time, the same question format and sampling methodology should be used.

SUMMARY

Valid, meaningful surveys provide an effective means for teams to obtain stakeholder input, but require much time and effort from team members. Before undertaking a survey, teams should consider whether the data can be collected in other ways. If surveys are necessary, it is important that potential sources of error be minimized. To achieve this, teams must ensure that people surveyed represent the true population under study, respondents accurately understand the questions asked, people are willing to participate in the survey process, and the results are analyzed objectively.

REFERENCES

American Association for Public Opinion Research. http://www.aapor.org.

Dillman, Don. (2000). *Mail and Internet Surveys: The Tailored Design Method.* New York, NY: John Wiley & Sons, Inc.

Light, Richard J., Judith D. Singer, and John B. Willett. (1990). *By Design: Planning Research on Higher Education.* Cambridge, MA: Harvard University Press.

Porter, Stephen R. (2004). "Pros and Cons of Paper and Electronic Surveys," *New Directions in Institutional Research* no 121:91–97.

Scheuren, Fritz. (2004). *What is a Survey?* Alexandria, VA: American Statistical Association.

Umbach, Paul D. (2005.) "Getting back to the basics of survey research," *New Directions in Institutional Research*, no. 127: 91–100.

HOW TO USE FOCUS GROUPS TO SOLICIT IDEAS AND FEEDBACK

Your organization provides services or products to varied constituencies, or as an institution of higher education or another not-for-profit service organization, you have many stakeholders—students, families, donors, local government, state legislators. You would like to get some feedback about how they see your organization and the services it provides. This chapter describes how to use focus groups to collect this information.

DEFINITION AND PURPOSE OF A FOCUS GROUP

A focus group is a qualitative research tool that involves the recording of responses and a detailed transcription from a one to two hour group discussion led by a facilitator. It provides a forum for soliciting ideas and feedback. The focus group discussion is guided by specific questions about a product, service, or organization. You can use focus groups to obtain in-depth knowledge by listening to participants as they share and compare their experiences, feelings, and opinions and gather more data in a shorter time than could be collected in individual interviews. The synergy created by a focus group can generate more than the sum of individual inputs. However, since the information is gathered through group discussion, it is generally not possible to quantify it. Also, the discussion may take on a life of its own as the group expands on questions and issues.

Focus groups can be used to:

- Analyze and improve products, services, or processes or identify, clarify, or correct a problem.
- Measure or evaluate a process to determine the current condition.
- Provide factual information as a guide in making decisions, replacing opinions, and focusing on data.
- Build a base of common knowledge about an issue or topic, especially about constituent needs and expectations.
- Evaluate the effects of change.

Focus groups can also be used as a preliminary stage in developing a survey, to determine what issues or questions to include or not include on the survey, and what choices or alternatives to offer as answers to the survey questions.

HOW TO BEGIN

Because of the nature of focus group discussions, adequate preparation is key. Since the facilitator will be guiding the discussion, it is useful to collaborate with the facilitator in developing the questions and making other preparations. Because the focus group discussion is based on anonymity, it is important to select a neutral facilitator—usually someone external to the unit or institution. The facilitator should also have expertise in focus group methodology, design, and process, so that he/she can keep the group on track without stifling discussion, and record all relevant information.

In advance, develop a discussion guide around the topic to be probed. In addition to the questions, the guide should include:

- An introduction to the topic and purpose
- Introduction of the moderator/facilitator
- Thanks to the participants
- Round robin introduction of the participants
- Review of the format—no wrong answers, anonymity regarding reporting of the discussion

- Closing comments, including a summary of key points, a reminder of optional future contact with the moderator/ facilitator to provide additional input, and information on access to and distribution of the collected data

In developing the questions, avoid questions that persuade, evaluate, or judge specific individuals, promote false or negative expectations, or propose activities contrary to institutional policies or practices.

Determine how to collect participant input. The simplest approach may be to record on chart paper, and if this is used, a second moderator/facilitator may be useful. If audio or video tape will be used, be sure to get participants' permission before the session begins.

The final product of the focus group(s) will be a written summary of the discussions. It is critical to decide during the planning phase to whom this report will be distributed.

Each focus group should consist of eight to ten participants. Consider which populations you would like to have input from. For example, in discussion of your advising process, you might want input from both the student and the faculty/advisor perspective. This might lead to two discussion groups, one of students and one of faculty/advisors. Or there might be a need for a group of traditional students and a group of adult students. The more homogeneous the background and perspectives of the participant population, the fewer groups will be needed; if additional discussions are not producing more new ideas, three or four focus groups may be sufficient. Within these target populations, select or invite a random sample of representatives.

The final step is to select a location for the discussions. It should be accessible and comfortable. Providing refreshments may serve as an incentive to those invited to attend, and may encourage them to participate once they arrive.

FACILITATING THE FOCUS GROUP

While a representative of the organization may begin the focus group session and introduce the facilitator, that representative will not be present for the discussion. During the focus group, the moderator/ facilitator will be responsible for:

- Beginning the discussion with welcome and background information

- Describing the meeting format and ground rules.
- Guiding the discussion with general questions, followed by specific questions
- Controlling interaction in the group
- Moving irrelevant discussion back on track
- Restarting discussion when the group "runs dry"
- Ensuring that groupthink doesn't stifle opinions that differ from the majority
- Discouraging overly dominant participants
- Engaging overly reticent participants
- Recording key points in the discussion
- Closing discussion with announcement of follow-up plans and thank-yous

THE FOCUS GROUP REPORT

The final product of the focus group(s) is a written summary of the focus group discussion(s), produced by the moderator/facilitator and distributed as determined during the planning. This report will include background information such as the number of focus groups, the number of participants, and the populations represented in the groups. The summary of the discussion should mention the difference in responses to the questions between different populations. What is not included in the report is any information that will make it possible to identify which participants made what comments.

ADVANTAGES AND DISADVANTAGES OF FOCUS GROUPS

There are many advantages to using focus groups. They can:

- Provide more information than interviews due to group interaction
- Help establish or enhance relationships between members of the group
- Identify new issues or questions researchers may not have thought to ask

- Provide believable results at reasonable cost
- Offset the tendency to rely too much on what's quantifiable

However, there are also disadvantages. Focus groups:

- Require more skill on the part of facilitators than do individual interviews
- Do not provide results that can be generalized to broader populations
- May have potentially unbalanced information and results because of group dynamics and lack of confidentiality and anonymity in the discussion

REFERENCES

Krueger, Richard. (1994). *Focus Groups: A Practical Guide for Applied Research.* Thousand Oaks, CA: Sage Publications, Inc.

Morgan, D.L. (1988). *Focus Groups as Qualitative Research.* Sage University Paper Series on Qualitative Research Methods. Vol. 19. Beverly Hills, CA: Sage Publications, Inc.

Simon, J.S. (1999). How to Conduct a Focus Group. Retrieved from http://www.tgci.com/magazine/How% 20to%20Conduct%20a%20Focus%20Group.pdf on October 12, 2007.

BENCHMARKING FOR INNOVATION AND IMPROVEMENT

WHY BENCHMARK?

Benchmarking can help you…

- Analyze and improve your processes
- Enhance performance
- Gather the information you need to assess your present and plan your future
- Identify some better approaches to accomplish your mission, vision, and goals

STARTING A BENCHMARKING EFFORT

What is benchmarking?

Robert Camp (1989) defines benchmarking as "the search for those best practices that will lead to the superior performance" of a unit or organization. It can help you to find effective practices at other organizations for services in which your institution is not providing the level of quality, satisfaction, or efficiency you would like to see. The emphasis is on studying the practices and processes of recognized leading organizations to find out how they do what they do, rather than gathering results and bottom line data and trying to match or beat those.

Benchmarking is not limited to the collection of numbers and comparison of averages, nor is it a one-time effort. It's not a test to see whether your unit is measuring up. It's a means to gather information and then target areas and processes for improvement.

With whom can you benchmark? What can you benchmark?

There are three types of benchmarking:

- Process benchmarking involves identification of best practices.
- Strategic benchmarking involves identifying emerging trends in a market or industry for strategic or resource planning.
- Comparative benchmarking is results oriented, and can be useful in setting stretch goals.

How can you deal with resistance to benchmarking?

Your organization may be doing well. The common perception may be that you're one of the best, and no one else provides exactly the same functions, services, or products that you do. However, while each unit and organization is unique, we share processes with other organizations, there is always the opportunity to be better, and someone else may just have a better way to do it. Your unit also needs to be able to meet the rising expectations of those who receive your products or services.

How does benchmarking relate to strategic and unit planning?

Benchmarking can be part of the initial stages of planning, as you assess current performance and set goals for improvement. It can also be part of the accomplishment of strategies, as you study outstanding organizations for alternative approaches to how your unit does its work.

- Internal benchmarking involves collecting comparative data from similar units within your organization. While this may be the easiest, data may be limited.

- Benchmarking with competitors involves comparison with similar organizations in the same field. Data collection may be difficult, but American Productivity and Quality Center's *Benchmarking Code of Conduct* may facilitate the exchange of information.
- Functional/generic benchmarking involves gathering information from an organization with the same or similar processes, although the organization may be in a different field. An example of this could be comparing your institution's online services with those of a bank.

What are the options for collecting benchmarking data?

While we often think that personal, face-to-face contact is necessary to benchmark, that is not always the case. Much information you are seeking may be available publicly, in news, trade, or professional journals, annual reports, or online databases. If you are gathering new information personally, you may be able to collect it through mailed written surveys or telephone interviews. If you gather new information, it is critical that you agree at the start regarding the confidentiality of the information, and you may want to plan a way to share the information gathered with all of your benchmarking partners.

THE PHASES OF BENCHMARKING

Like many other organizational initiatives, effective benchmarking begins with preparation, and moves through several phases.

Phase One: Identifying and examining your own processes

- Which processes are most critical to your success?
- Which processes provide the greatest opportunities for improvement?
- How are these processes currently performed? Can you map the processes?

- How is the performance of these processes currently measured? Can measures be developed if they are not currently in place?

Phase Two: Identifying the organizations with which you will benchmark, and how data will be collected

- What organizations or units are known within your professional network or field as highly effective in regard to the services, products, or processes you would like to benchmark?
- What organizations have been recognized publicly for their accomplishments in the services, products, or processes you would like to benchmark?
- What questions would you like answered based on your analysis of your own processes?
- Do you need personal contact to get these answers, or can it be provided in writing?

Phase Three: Collecting and analyzing the data

- Once data is collected, the task is to compare performance levels and practices, and identify performance gaps in your organization.
- Where are the similarities and differences in practices and processes?
- What can you apply or adapt in your unit from the other organizations' approaches ?
- What ideas for new approaches, services, or products are triggered by what you learn about other organizations' approaches?

Phase Four: Establishing targets to close the gaps and developing action plans to reach those targets

- What are your future performance goals and measures for the targeted processes?
- What innovations or improvements do you want to implement to reach these targets?
- What support or challenges exist for these changes?

- Who should be involved in planning and carrying out this implementation to maximize its success?

Phase Five: Implementing the action plans and tracking progress toward the goals

- What are the milestones for implementation?
- How frequently should you measure performance? Monthly? Quarterly? Are there seasonal or semester variations?

One of the biggest risks is having too many benchmarking partners and collecting too much information. One approach is to first gather preliminary information from a larger number of prospective partners (a broad approach), and then use that information to identify a smaller set of partners with which to examine key processes in more detail (a focused approach).

Another challenge is to plan your benchmarking effort so that you have a quick turnaround from collecting data to setting goals.

For a successful benchmarking effort, include:

- A systematic, carefully defined approach
- A candid assessment of your own organization
- A willingness to learn from others
- A long-term approach

RESOURCES

American Productivity and Quality Center. *Benchmarking Code of Conduct.* http://www.apqc.org/ Retrieved October 5, 2007.

Camp, Robert C. (1989). *Benchmarking—The Search for Industry Best Practices That Lead to Superior Performance.* Milwaukee, WI: ASQC Quality Press.

Camp, Robert C. (1995). *Business Process Benchmarking: Finding and Implementing Best Practices.* Milwaukee, WI: ASQC Quality Press.

McNair, C. J. CMA, and Kathleen H. J. Leibfried. (1992). *Benchmarking: A Tool for Continuous Improvement.* Essex Junction, VT: Omneo Oliver Wright Publications, Inc.

Patterson, J. G. (1996). *Benchmarking Basics: Looking for a Better Way.* Menlo Park, CA: Crisp Publications, Inc.

Spendolini, Michael J. (1992). *The Benchmarking Book.* New York, NY: American Management Association.

United States National Institute of Standards and Technology, and Baldrige National Quality Award. http://www.nist.gov/ Retrieved October 5, 2007.

CONCLUSION

The foundation for integrating planning, assessment, and improvement is built on analysis and effective communication. From the beginning, be clear about your reasons for investing time and other resources in the projects and initiatives. Identify what you expect as outcomes, and what will define success. Involve and engage those people who, through both their expertise and knowledge and their support for the work involved, are needed to ensure success. Then determine how to keep the rest of the organization informed as you move forward.

A wide range of approaches and tools should be considered in your initial planning and analysis. Efficiency and effectiveness apply here. Resources are always limited, so don't do more than is needed for your specific project. Ensure that the approaches and tools you select are the best fit for the goals of your initiative and the people involved. You have more in your tool kit than the proverbial hammer, and each project should not look like the proverbial nail.

Once the initiative has been implemented, two key items remain. First, provide recognition for all those involved in the development and implementation. They were probably working on this in addition to their regular responsibilities, and they made the time to make the project succeed. Those outside of the team will see from the recognition that special projects and initiatives are becoming part of the organization's culture.

Second, gather data after the implementation to document and publicize the results. This will demonstrate that work on planning, assessment, or improvement teams is an investment in both the future of the organization and the professional development of the team members. It provides a tangible return, in contrast to time-consuming meetings that produce few results.

As people move from the cost to the investment concept for planning and improvement initiatives, your efforts will gain momentum.

We hope this book will help you to move your plans off the shelf and into weekly and daily activities, move assessment from an ending score to a guide for future goals and actions, and move process improvement, innovation, and reengineering from isolated events to the means to implement the goals and strategies in your college's or university's plan.

GLOSSARY

Assessment. Using data to identify areas for improvement, and to track and analyze progress toward the achievement of vision and goals.

Cause. Reason for ineffectiveness or inefficiency of a process. When the cause is addressed, the process is improved.

Continuous Quality Improvement (CQI). A people-based management system that applies to all levels of an organization. Designed to continually improve the performance of that organization, its focus is on exceeding customer expectations by using data to incrementally improve key processes.

Customer. Anyone—internal or external—who receives a product or service, such as students, parents, alumni, and employees.

Effectiveness. The extent to which a process meets the needs of its stakeholders.

Efficiency. The extent to which a process makes good use of resources.

Goals. Broad statements describing how you will reach your vision, answering the questions "How will we know when we've arrived?" and "How will we get there?"

IMPROVE Model. A model used at Penn State for improvement; an application of the scientific method based on the Plan-Do-Study-Act (PDSA) cycle developed by Walter Shewhart in the 1930s.

Improvement. An approach to enhance organizational performance through the use of data-based decision making, process improvement, and stakeholder involvement.

Mission. A statement of purpose, answering the question "What is our primary purpose?"

Performance Measures. Specific data that enable you to determine when you've achieved your goals.

Planning. A process for guiding future-oriented decisions, setting priorities, and allocating resources. Many departments make planning an ongoing activity that involves stakeholders.

Process. A series of steps taken to accomplish a task.

Process map. A diagram of the steps or activities in a process; also known as a flowchart.

Stakeholder. Anyone who has an interest in a product or service or is otherwise affected by the service, such as customers, government agencies, businesses, and taxpayers.

Strategies and Action Plans. Specific, detailed statements that describe how you will achieve your goals. Generally list what will be done, how and when it will happen, and who is responsible.

Supplier. Source of the material and/or information input to a process, which may be internal or external to the organization.

Systems. In a system, all functions, activities, and processes are interdependent. Focusing on the interactions between parts, rather than focusing on improving the parts alone, improves the system.

Team. A group of people with shared responsibility for a common goal.

Values. Basic precepts about what is important in your institution, answering the question "What are our assumptions and beliefs?"

Vision. A clear and compelling overall description of the desired future state, answering the question "Where does our unit want to go?"

NOTES